Share Faire Famous

Share Faire Famous

Stephanie Henson

Oh MG Press

This is a work of fiction. All of the characters, organizations, and events portrayed in this novel are either of the author's imagination or are used fictitiously.

ISBN 979-8-8691-9307-0

 Publishing by OhMG Press, by arrangement with Ingram Content Group One Ingram Blvd., La Vergne, Tennessee 37086, US. Distributions by arrangement with Ingram Content Group One Ingram Blvd., La Vergne, Tennessee 37086, US.

Printed in the U.S.A

First OhMG Printing , June 2024

Share Faire Famous

To my friend Dave Latini - Real is hard to find in Middle School but you were the real deal! You are missed by many.

1

June | 5th Grade Graduation

Sparks are going off inside my body, mini fireworks burning up the little patience I have left. It's worse than when I was in line for the Rollercoaster of Doom, and it took forever for my turn. The Rollercoaster of Doom has nothing on this! We are going to be so late. I mean, it's only my 5th Grade Graduation! Beaming sunlight is giving off a relentless heat and I'm sure all of the close parking spaces have been taken, which means a long sweaty walk is in store for me. Why does it have to be so hot? Today of all days! Couldn't Mother Nature give us a break? Ugh! My name is Marshall Hope, and I am about to be an official middle schooler. I just have to make it to the ceremony and actually graduate 5th grade first, but my mom is making it extremely difficult.

“Laura, what are you doing? We are way behind schedule. Let’s go!" my dad roared.

“I’m packing the last of the equipment," she shot back.

Aahh, the camera! Of course! Even the accessories took extra effort to corral, and everyone knows that camera is her lifeline. If you hooked that camera up to a heart monitor, I bet you it would have a pulse! The camera is the window into people’s lives that allows my mom to peek behind the curtain to see what others do not. She lives, breathes, and writes about what the camera provides access to. She simply could not function without it, as an Internet Blogger, who chronicles the details and happenings of everyday life in and out of our family. Plus, there was no possible scenario that would have me graduating without that thing pointed directly in my overexposed face.

"Ready," she yelled.

Bumping and thumping in and out of my seat over each mile, it's hard to concentrate. Being in elementary school is Easy Street! The glowing spotlight of my life up until this point is about to dim. To say that I am nervous about middle school is an understatement of epic proportions. I have no idea how the students will react to me and my "status." My anxiety about everything changing has been on full blast like shuttles taking off to the beyond. Launching myself into outer space actually sounds like a more appealing option than going to Middle School, right about now. I keep worrying about the other kids.

I have been the focus of attention my entire life, so I should be used to it. But now the reality that all eyes are sure to be on me today is annoying. Lines of cars are like sardines and a can opener is necessary to fit into a spot.

Like a mini stunt man flinging himself out of a careening car, I jumped out before the vehicle even had a chance to stop. Racing towards the cramped crowd, we made it just in time to hear the opening remarks from our principal.

My best friend and neighbor Caden sucked on a lollipop in the middle of the jam-packed group. Classic Caden. Waving emphatically, while his cheeks hollowed out from sucking the last bits of his treat, it was comforting to see a friendly face.

A white tent overhead provided little shelter from the rising temperatures. The students were wedged in the chairs with no wiggle room to spare. My legs will fall asleep before the audience does at this bore-fest. The microphone boomed, "What if there was a portal within all of the apps you use that allows you to glimpse your future self? Would you be okay with the choices you made? Would you like what you see? Where do you want to be 10 years from now? Do you see it?"

Wow, adults sure do like to lecture a lot. What is with all of the questions? Principal Bloom is rambling on and on about the future. Dude, you know we are kids, right? We don't even know what we're eating after this, so have no clue what we will be doing years from now. My immediate future consists of taking off this uncomfortable button-down shirt since the tag has been itching my neck for the past hour like fleas on a Beagle. Early June days in PA can be brutal with weather and today is no exception, so I'm about two seconds from shapeshifting into a puddle monster at this outdoor event. *#Swampy*

Balloons danced in the wind and fragrant flowers flanked the aisles and permeated the air. Despite the celebratory atmosphere, Mr. Bloom's obvious intent is to scare everyone silly about the fears of adulthood. At least that is what it sounded like to me. With his long finger pointing wildly and his voice fluctuating in tone, I'm surprised he didn't throw in warnings about the effects of looking directly into the sun or the dangers of black ice in the winter. He's a real killjoy sometimes!

Out of the corner of my almond shaped eye, my dad Ben is giving me the death stare, so I better pay attention. Not one to mess around, Dad has no tolerance for ignorance. He has the intensity of a thousand burning suns so he can give this event a run for the money. He might even quiz me after the ceremony on what life lessons Principal Bloom outlined in his speech, so I cocked my head to the side and turned up my ear to make sure I heard every word.

Bloom's Basics to Flourish in Life:

1. Always be honest.
2. Be true to yourself.
3. Respect yourself and others.
4. Win with grace, lose with grace.
5. Forgiveness is important and a secret ingredient in the recipe for happiness.

Principal Bloom believes as we get older there will be choices that could impact our lives as adults. It's a perfect opportunity for him to introduce the crowd to the legend of Ethan Fox. Although he never mentioned him by name, we all knew who he was talking about. #*Infamous*

Ethan attended our school several years ago and was a talented student/athlete. Tall in stature and idolized as a baseball phenom, Ethan had it all. Rumor has it Ethan and his friends got very into the idea of being "Share Faire Famous." Everyone who has a phone knows about "Share Faire." It is a social media-networking platform for people to make short videos and post them. The creators developed it to be a daily festival filled with different challenges, games, dances, and contests. The app's users are all sorts of characters who wanted to be a part of a unique online community. Others, though, only created content in the pursuit of fame and fortune. Suddenly, for Ethan, baseball got pushed aside for this new hobby. The stunts were of

Marvel superhero magnitude, and he pretty much burned that baseball bridge with a flamethrower and a fractured pitching arm. *#TrueStory*

The energy instantly changed, and the crowd rustled uncomfortably. I could make out whispers about "Hope" and "Share Faire." "There's the camera . . . I'm sure this will be online later today. . . does she have no shame?" Catty chatter rippled through the crowd.

My mother Laura shuffled around in her seat, however that darn camera she was holding was steady and never broke the frame. Hundreds of curious eyeballs leered in my direction. Running fidgety fingers through my messy brown hair, the sweat beads collected on my brow either from the heat of the mercury or the heat of the moment. Thankfully, there was Caden, his lollipop gone and now chomping on a wad of gum. It's rare you'd ever see him without some sort of snack, he is a trip! The girls all have heart eyes for my charming best friend. We play soccer together and are on our Xbox's way too much. He is also a human garbage disposal who can devour an entire gallon of ice cream in one sitting with no consequence. I'm always amazed by the sheer amount of food he is able to fit in his lean body. I was positive that by the time we reached Middle School, he would weigh about 500 pounds. But, no.

With a mischievous glint in his eye, he winked at me, then broke the stifling tension by leaning almost horizontally in his chair. He let out an obscene snort and pretended to fall asleep in the middle of the student section. However, his chair slipped out from under him, and he went crashing to the ground mimicking a meteor plunging towards Earth. The candy he was saving for later fell out of his pockets and blanketed the grass around him.

Fellow Fifth graders were in fits of frenzy. It was like a pinata explosion of activity. Rebounding like Lebron, Caden composed himself and let out a quick, "I'm awake," and waved unashamedly towards the packed parent gallery.

Caden's mom's forehead wrinkled as she whisper-yelled loud enough for heads to turn, "Caden Matthew Lowe, are you for real right now?" Her hands were clenched so tight her knuckles shook, as a flush of embarrassment bloomed across her tight and rigid expression. "This kid has done it again!"

Red in the face and holding back tears of laughter, I nearly had to check my bladder and my khakis! But my dad glared my way, and it was no secret he was definitely going to ground me until I was forty-six! So, I sucked it all in, looked straight ahead, and put on my most serious face.

It was not enough though. There he was - my dad - aggressively mouthing the words, "Pay Attention, Marshall!" Drenched in sweat, the Ghost Rider's tears no doubt, he was either ignited by fury over my behavior or it was just that warm out here under the tent, an incubator of fire. Late Spring and Summer in the Philadelphia area are no joke!

Parents and students listened intently but the heat festered. The lack of airflow was borderline suffocating, so event programs became makeshift fans in an attempt to provide relief in the moment. Even our Mascot "Woofie" faded into a mess of furry fleece. Leaning against an empty seat, he went down without warning, and was OUT, taking the chair with him! Thank goodness the school nurse was on hand to hydrate and bring him back to life.

#StayCool

Wrap it up, Big Guy.

"What would you do?" Principal Bloom questioned as he swatted some bees away from his damp face. "If given the chance, would you take the easy way out? Or would you do the right thing?"

"Every action and every choice leads to another action and choice. What lies ahead and where you want to be depends on your ability to dream big but also work hard. You are in control of your future."

Mr. Bloom flailed and wailed as more bees swarmed around him. His animated movements made him look as if he was trying to replicate the newest Share Faire dance! But I was too distracted to care. I began playing with my hands—twisting and pulling my thumbs—as the worries crept back in. Why did I suddenly feel so out of control? Is my anxiety obvious? Being that I can't sit still, it wouldn't take Xray vision in this case. Not only will the kids know who I am at my new middle school, so will their friends, and their friends' friends, not to mention parents and teachers! If they knew the internal struggles of someone in my position, maybe they would be more forgiving.

After his speech concluded and the bees retreated to their hive, one by one, students strutted across the stage to receive their 5th Grade Graduation Certificate. My thoughts swirled in my head while I tried to figure out what my future holds. I'm not sure who I am but everyone else seems to have an opinion.

I was snapped out of my crashing brain waves when my name was called, "Congratulations to Marshall Hope." Aware of the crowd gawking at me, I shook Mr. Bloom's hand, self-conscious about my moist grip, and held my diploma to pose for a photo. Confetti cannons exploded and hundreds of tiny multicolored tissue paper pieces gradually rained down on the attendees. That majestic moment in time would later receive over a million likes.

You see, my name is Marshall Goode Hope. I am going into 6th Grade, and I am "Share Faire Famous."

2

The Early Years

So, you are probably wondering why I am famous. Well, when I was almost a year old, my mom did a lot of blogging about “Share Faire." She promoted it on her personal page and did reaction pieces to many of the first videos on the platform.

I guess that is where my Share Faire story begins. At ten months old, I really didn't do much, but I was very photogenic and expressive. A rosy cheeked cherub with a face full of cheerios can get hundreds of likes - who knew? Boppin’ and chompin’ babies are a vibe online! My mom posted videos of me doing simple everyday things like . . .

breathing. It was important for her to document all of our growing up milestones but since I am the last child and her only son, I basically grew up with a camera in my face. When I was little, I called it the magical memory box. From the time it took my mom to point, click, and shoot, I was up on a screen. I thought my mom was top of her class at wizarding school!

I am not gifted by any means and definitely fall headfirst into the category of no life changing talent, but big opportunity. That year, Share Faire had a "Cutest Baby" contest where the winner got to be featured in a popular online baby magazine. Thousands of babies entered. I am actually named after the famous Supreme Court Justice Thurgood Marshall, so mom dressed me like a judge. Sporting a mini black robe, gavel in hand, and wearing dad's black glasses, I transformed into "Baby Justice Marshall" - and I won. Overnight I became the internet's most famous baby. There were even memes that included my photo, “The verdict is in, Justice Marshall wins” and “Marshall Rules” were shared over and over across the interwebs.

If that notoriety was not enough, there was my head. A dazzling planet sized phenomenon in a galaxy all its own. Let’s just say I had to grow into it, and it took some time! My head kept me off balance for the first year of my life.

So, sometimes when I tried to do new things, I would topple over. Sit up - topple over. Stand Up - topple over. Walk - topple over. Sneeze - topple over.

A doctor once told my parents, "Don't worry too much, he will grow into that noggin." Gee, thanks doc.

My mom’s videos kept getting more and more views, likes, and comments. The attention was all consuming. It got to where everyone thought they were an expert on my development. They knew my name, my sister's names, why we were named, and had opinions on our names. You name it!

For years, I was sent packages from followers on my birthday, for holidays, and for no reason at all. *#Swag*

My sisters got some gifts too, but they did not like being photographed as much as I did. Ruby, my oldest sister, had a shy side as a kid. She has grown out of it for the most part, but she was never natural in front of the camera. Annie, the middle child, was a tornado who left a path of sports related debris wherever she landed. My mom couldn't keep up. Unlike my sisters, I was easy and sat still. It really wasn't much of a choice for me to be featured online but I did not mind. My growth both in personality and looks was free for all to see. *#GlowUp*

When I look back sometimes, I can't believe my goofy little grin garnered so much attention. Honestly, I'd describe myself as average with a twist. My light brown hair is common, but my eyes are dark chestnut, almost black, and my wispy eyelashes are the envy of most middle-aged women. My Cabbage Patch kid-like quality probably contributed to the starstruck admiration. I brought nostalgia to the table and spoon fed it to the masses.

Mom's posts and blogs are super popular and timely. She even wrote about Ethan Fox and his ultimate career-ending stunt gone wrong. Okay, I know you must be dying to know the deets. Ethan thought it would be a good idea to propel himself off a roof like Spiderman, try to land on a trampoline, so he could then web sling himself over to a diving board, where - from there - for the grand finale - he would double flip into a pool. *#NoSpideySenses*

Legend had it, you could hear the chorus of encouragement from blocks away, "Ethan Jump, Ethan Jump, Ethan Jump!" Endless clapping, pounding, and yelling shook the yard with a rumble. Party lights shone bright around the house and pizza boxes littered the lawn.

"Come on E, you got this. What's the worst that could happen?" the crowd urged.

Famous last words from his so-called friends. Well, Ethan never made it past the first obstacle. After his lofty leap from the roof, his knees buckled upon hitting the trampoline and with violent force he yeeted himself right into the pool fence. He did achieve instant viral infamy but never threw a ball across home plate again. My mom did an in-depth analysis on what went wrong and came to the conclusion that he knew nothing about physics or common sense. *#Wipeout*

Share Faire was and still is extremely popular. There are many famous Share Faire creators who have thousands to millions of followers. They basically dictate what's in and out in fashion, music, movies, and books. Everyone wants to be an influencer. Ring lights are a must, and your hashtag game needs to be tight! People from all over the world record themselves doing anything from trendy dances to just being themselves. The more likes and followers you have, the more relevant you become.

People from all over the place knew me. When I started preschool the kids called me “Justice Marshall” or that “Share Faire kid." I didn't really have to work very hard to make friends. The other kids just wanted to be around me. I didn't understand why at the time, but I do now. It was like that with every passing grade.

By the time I made it to where I am now, things were easy peasy. I am not saying that I don’t work hard in school. My dad would not allow bad grades. My A’s are straight and my cooperation skills are on point! Nothing was too tough to handle in elementary school. Everyone knew me, everything was easy, and now everything is about to change.

3

July | 6th Grade Orientation

It is the morning of Middle School orientation. How is it even possible? Fifth Grade graduation was a month ago, but it feels like yesterday. We are in the throes of summer break but for incoming sixth graders who are only 11 and 12 years old, the torture starts early. Orientation day consists of building tours, meeting teachers, assemblies on rules and the ever-dreaded locker trials. You seriously need a magic wand and a rabbit in a hat in order to open a stupid locker! *#Facts*

Weston Middle School is where I will spend the next three years. Sixth grade is a big deal for everyone. Leaving the sheltered life of Woodside Elementary School is scary. Familiar halls lined with art projects, walls covered in handprints, and lemon fumes from the cafeteria are now a memory.

Most of the kids who were at the Woodside graduation will be at orientation today. But there are other schools in our district that will feed into it too, which means - all new sets of eyes locked on me. Or who they think I might be. Good luck figuring that one out. Growing up on an app makes it hard for people to know what's real vs. what's staged. Looking back on some moments from my childhood, I have a hard time distinguishing if I was really happy in a photo or if it was one of the 10 takes my mom took to get the moment just right. It also makes it hard for me to know who's real vs. who is fake. Sometimes kids just want to be friends with me because they think I'll make them famous too.

Caden will be with me at orientation - safety in numbers. Official schedules will not be released until the end of summer, but we know we have a decent shot at being together in some of the classes and in the same Hall since they are grouped alphabetically. I waited for him to come out so we could leave. Coming down the gray slate steps with a corndog in one hand and a coke in the other, Caden emerged seemingly unfazed about today. What kind of breakfast is that? Who eats a corndog before a school event? Typical Caden! I'm sure his stomach is like a fart in a pressure cooker right now.

We chatted on the way about video games, but I was in my own world. Today was the moment of truth - will my Share Faire fame impact my time at Weston? Will I be able to have a normal middle school experience or will I have to deal with invasions to my pride and privacy from minute one? I am not even sure who I am at this point. I could just embrace the fame and popularity. Or I can try to carve out my own path, on my own terms. *#LifeChoices*

My nerves were having a party in my tummy as we turned the corner and pulled into the Weston Middle School parking lot. Caden jumped right out of the car, hurdled over an orange cone like a track star, without a bit of hesitation. Confident and sure of himself, Caden never has a hard time navigating his way around a crowd. I barely got one foot out of the door before he was canoodling with some swooning girls in front of the building.

People are drawn to Caden like peanut butter to jelly. He's charismatic, popular, and fun to hang out with. His blonde curly hair touches the tips of his eyelids that house ocean blue eyes. He's tan year-round, and looks like he could grace the cover of a Surfer magazine - so he glides through life. No punishment for the graduation stunt, obviously! His mom even thinks he walks on water which is why she didn't end up grounding him either. *#Get-Out-of-Jail-Free-Card*

Unsure of myself, I looked down at the floor as my feet dragged toward the auditorium for the first session of the day. When I managed to make eye contact, glares and stares from the other students shot directly into my skull. The kids, some who I knew, others who were new, surely had seen my mom's latest post from Woodside's graduation. I can still hear the pop of the confetti cannon. Photos from my preschool graduation intertwined with the elementary graduation footage. Every detail of my life thus far has been accounted for at Share Faire. Literally morphing from baby to preteen with the graduation march as an exclamation point, the post was one of her most viral, along with the first time I actually walked without falling on my face. *#NoFail*

Once the first presentation was over, a slew of kids crowded the stark hallways, as we toured the main wing of

Weston. I was not so worried about the building. I had been there before for my older sister's events. It was split into three grade level wings and each wing had four main hallways, numbered 1-4. The homerooms are normally grouped by last name. Since my last name starts with "H," it was likely that I'd be in Hall 2, right in the center of everything, sort of like my life up to this point.

Sun streaking through the large skylights overhead cast shadows throughout the building. The rustic floors outfitted with red brick pavers led to ramps in different sections of the school. Since it's summer, the bare walls looked sad as the teachers have not yet been in to arrange their classrooms with banners of art in every color of the rainbow. Lonely chairs sat atop empty desks, yet, by contrast, exuberant students were hustling and bustling down the halls, taking notes, and trying to figure out where they were.

One group of girls in particular caught my attention. They were huddled together and seemed to think very highly of themselves, often fluffing their hair and fixing their faces with makeup and admiring their handiwork. Light bounced off their mini mirrors and reflected confidence in every direction. One girl mouthed something in my direction, but I could not make it out.

As usual, much attention was given to Caden with his tousled locks and diamond smile. The feisty flock of females surrounded him with thirst in their eyes. We got separated so I don't know if they kidnapped him, swallowed him whole, or if he managed to escape.

Some of the middle school teachers volunteered to escort us around the building and to various classrooms. There was no line, just herds of tween cattle clumped together comparable to the running of the bulls in Spain. Bodies bumped down the walkways, all that was missing was a red scarf. I felt a piece of paper enter my hand. It was a note. Someone managed to pass me a note unnoticed in the crowd. How? When I got to my seat, I unfolded the tiny, crinkled piece of paper. An ominous message was scribbled in cursive:

Beware SHARE SCARE!

What the what?

Suddenly, the air was sucked out of the room. A shiver went down my spine and my stomach felt as if I were going upside down on the world's biggest roller coaster, one that would dwarf the Roller Coaster of Doom! Who gave me this? What was this supposed to mean? Someone clearly had it out for me. I feared something like this could happen. Not everyone is into Share Faire. And now someone is clearly not into me. *#NotSoSecretAdmirer*

While people generally love Share Faire and the opportunities that it yields, there is a large group of people who really don't appreciate the app's creators and the fame they are able to achieve, almost instantly with little talent.

As a result, there is a lot of hate that goes around, and you have to be able to deal with that. *#HatersGonnaHate*

Not only do I have no idea who I am at this point, I have no idea who wrote me the note. Come to think of it, there have been a lot of anonymous comments on my mom's Share Faire page lately with the same message:

Beware SHARE SCARE!

The hairs stood up on my arms at those words. It must be the same person from today's orientation wreaking havoc on my mom's page. We are used to negativity, but this somehow feels as if it crosses a line. This is my school. It's not just some idiot spitting nonsense out into the universe. It's too close to home. This is my life!

Beware SHARE SCARE!

So, let me get this straight: not only do I have to start a new school and figure out who the heck I am outside of being "Justice Marshall," but now I have a bully too? Couldn't someone just send me some fan mail and call it a day? Is it not enough that the physical changes overcome me on the regular and the mounting anxiety could blaze a trail to Mount Everest? It's a little too much for a 12-year-old some days.

Yet, I've decided not to tell Mom about what happened. I know, I know. First, she'd be worried then would completely come undone. There is enough going on without adding in Mama drama.

4

Family Ties

It's crazy how three little words can knock your world off center. **Beware SHARE SCARE!**

Over-analyzing the little pieces of evidence I have; it is obviously someone I did not know. I have been going to school with the same group of friends since preschool and none of them would do this. We were a team, even before Principal Bloom spoke directly into my soul on graduation day.

I think Mr. Bloom spoke to my mom's soul as well since she was, in fact, the reason I am internet famous.

There was a reason she self-consciously wiggled her butt at my graduation.

There are days where I resent the unwanted attention and today is that day.

"Come on Marshall, smile for the camera" is a phrase I hear in my sleep.

Magical Memory Box my . . .

Laura

As an Internet blogger who loves theater, music, and all things entertainment, my mom Laura is up on every single trend and hashtag known to man. Perhaps that is an exaggeration, but pop culture is that lady's life and she had a hand in putting me right in the middle of it.

"Mom," I called out.

"Do you know where my soccer cleats went? I left them by the door last night when I got back from practice."

"I'm in the middle of doing a voice over for a new client, hang on." she said.

Right! This client who had been begging her to include me in a Share Faire video for a new line of baby care products. Um, do they not realize that I am 12 years old and not an actual baby anymore? If they want, I can show them the fuzz of hair starting to form on my upper lip, or send them a box of my old pacifiers, perhaps I can email them a copy of my birth certificate. This happens all the time, I should be used to it, but it bugs me big time that most people still think I am a toddler or a cartoon version of a growing boy.

Emerging from behind her lens, "Marshall, I put all of your soccer stuff in the garage. First, everything stunk to high heaven and secondly, nothing was in the right place. We were given those racks from one of my clients to use for situations just like this. They are not called "Sport Ports" for fun, they serve a purpose. Welcome to your house, buddy - live here long?" *#MyBad*

Oh that sarcastic tone. That's my mom, witty and biting. I swear for the first three years of my life, I didn't know what my mother actually looked like. I only saw a glimpse of her from behind the camera she was always positioning. I get it, she loved chronicling every little detail of our lives. I always wondered though, by documenting it, was she really living it? She took every photo, but was never in one. She was always setting up the perfect memories but never experienced them, firsthand. Everything she captured was a moment in time, but time she spent recording.

My mother did not have much of anything growing up and certainly did not have stacks of photos or videos to look through that celebrated her life. Her home life was very unstable. Like a table with one leg that holds a stack of problems, the more you add to it, eventually it will tip.

She and my Aunt Gabby were often left alone. Two little girls wandering hand and hand through life, they did not know their father very well. He drifted and made occasional appearances in their lives but ultimately went back to whatever nonsense was plaguing him that day. My Grandmom was a gem and held them together. She was a School Attendance Secretary before she passed away. She worked very hard to support her girls and often took odd jobs to make ends meet. My mom is still haunted by her childhood.

"Marshall," she once said, "My family's home was a shoebox with no shoes. Small, empty, and sad. So help me God, it would be different for us."

She vowed that whenever she had a family of her own, they would be shown unending affection, love, acceptance, and security in their family unit. And we did.

Before she had us kids, she worked in the marketing department for a pharmaceutical company. Snore-a-pa-looza. She didn't love it but did it because she thought she had to build a career to build her bank account. Society has certain standards but my mom drums to her own beat.

When we came along, she was able to stay home and pursue her lifelong dream, to write. She started her own blog that initially started as reactions to daily news, and Internet gossip. My mom is hilarious and always has a clever take. Her perspective had changed since becoming a mother, so she was able to invoke her trademark humor and sarcasm into every word she wrote.

Her blog eventually got traction and her articles were soon shared all over the Internet. Everything she does, she does for our family. My dad was proud.

Ben

My dad is a little more traditional than mom. Most of the time he kind of resembles Clark Kent before he turns into Superman. Strait-laced and kind of nerdy, Dad is quiet by nature unless he has a reason not to be. His fuse can short circuit in an instant, as evidenced by his thermonuclear level flare of irritation at graduation. When he was my age, he aspired to be on the Supreme Court. He clearly had zero fun things as a kid. His aspirations paid off though and now he's a successful lawyer with a full caseload. Dad's mantra is "Pick a lane, work hard, and have a path in life to attain goals."

My dad is built differently. He comes from a household where they actually set the table with good plates (not paper!), had utensils placed in the right order, complete with linen napkins and sterling silver utensils! *#Blessed*

His upbringing was very normal and stable. His parents (my grandparents) both had successful law careers, so they never really worried about money. They certainly never had to worry about where a meal would come from or if the lights would be on when they returned home at the end of the day. My dad has great sympathy and empathy for my mom's experiences. He just wants to take care of her and make her feel loved. My grandparents feel the same.

My father is a scholar, not blue collar. While my mom doesn't understand my dad's compulsion over "dad things" like the garbage and CNBC, he doesn't understand my mother's fascination with celebrity. They are the definition of opposites attract. Saturday mornings for mom are made for British accents while dancing around to the Mary Poppins musical soundtrack whereas Dad works in the garage listening to Country music. On Sunday mornings my dad drinks his coffee and reads the Wall Street Journal behind thick rimmed glasses. Whereas, Mom gulps bottomless mimosas and reads People Magazine while wearing Duchess inspired headwear . . . you get the point. They met at a party. My mom is a social butterfly and dad is a social hermit crab.

Ruby and Annie

I have two older sisters who are also named after Justices. While Dad was in charge of picking our first names, my mother chose our middle names to inspire and reinforce her beliefs in the world. Due to her upbringing, mom was an emotional escape artist. She immersed herself in wishes and looked for signs in life such as a penny heads up or a four-leaf clover. This led to her being whimsical by nature, someone who has total trust in the universe, and often relies on the stars to solidify her plans.

As a kid, she threw notes into the wind. Little transcripts of her heart that contained confessions of love and declarations of her wildest dreams. Only later did she consider the possibility that she was littering the streets with her daily duties of good, but her faith convinced her that they never touched the ground. Our middle names were her guiding lights in life, plus, it all sounded pretty hoppin with our last name being Hope.

My sister Ruby Faith is sixteen and named after the late Ruth Bader Ginsburg. My second older sister Annie's given name is Sandra Love Hope, after Sandra Day O'Connor. Ruth Bader Ginsburg was a lawyer who, early in her career, took a special interest in women's rights. Sandra Day O'Connor was the first female Justice on the Supreme

Court. The names fit. My sisters are excellent representations of what those trailblazers stood for. *#GirlPower*

Why did they not call my sister Sandy, one might wonder? Well, my mom did not want her name to be associated with a destructive hurricane that hit the NJ coast years ago. We lost our beach house in that storm and had to completely rebuild. It was a rough time. Since my mom is a walking musical production, she always imagined having a daughter named after her favorite - little orphan Annie. I wish I could tell you that our names are the strangest thing about my family. They are not.

Our family is on the internet. When you live out loud and give people permission to access your life, they take it. No signs of forced entry, yet it's a robbery. Some strange things about our family:

We live in a zoo enclosure. A clear, glass exhibitionists cage, of sorts. OK not really - but people see us. All of the time. All hours of the day. On tablets, on phones, on computers. People know everything about us. Period. Done. That's it. Strange. Thanks, Mom.

There are no secrets. People know Ruby won a Spelling Bee in 4th Grade. They knew when I pooped on the potty for the first time - greeeaaattt - and they were aware of what happened the first time Annie noticed someone ogling us with a camera while on vacation. She power walked right up with a high-pitched howl - a four-year-old full of resounding rage - and wailed "STRANGER DANGER " to whoever came too close. To this day, she's not really a people person. *#Baddie*

Speaking of Annie, she is thirteen, starting 8th grade, and still feisty. Little did my mother know that her mood changes could feel like a catastrophic act of nature. Annie is very athletic and plays anything with a stick (field hockey, ice hockey, and lacrosse). She is a year-round athlete and lives for sports. She will be there as I start my new school. We are close but not nearly as close as I am with Ruby. Ruby has been my cheerleader and protector my entire life. Don't get me wrong, she loves Annie, but they fight, as sisters tend to do; over clothes, over food, over breathing the same air! It's normal sister on sister crime.

"Seriously, Ruby! Does it take a year to shower, shave, and do your hair?" Annie argues.

"Coming from someone who looks like a Ringtail who slept under turf blankets at the lacrosse field, you absolutely have no clue!" Ruby barked back.

"Don't drown in the storm drain, Pennywise!" Annie cracked.

"Try not to look like a rabid raccoon, Annie!" Ruby retaliated.

"GIRLS - Knock it off NOW!" Dad shouted from his office.

Female mood swings! With Ruby and me it's different. There is a special bond between an older sister and a younger brother, and we definitely have it. Maybe it is because of our age difference. We are not too close to get on each other's nerves but not too far apart that we are out of orbit. With her long wavy caramel tinted hair, milk chocolate brown eyes and inviting smile, Ruby looks like me and is approachable and friendly to everyone, well almost everyone. *#SorryAnnie*

Ruby is very into activism and has been on the Student Council since middle school and will campaign again this coming year. There isn't an environmental club, anti-bullying event, or fundraising activity for underprivileged students that she is not a part of in school. If that is not enough, Ruby is also a gifted artist and loves working at the local art association summer camps every year. She is always the first person I run to when I need help or advice, and with this being such a big weekend, I'm sure I will sprint to her soon.

Ruby was the brain, Annie was the muscle, and I was something else entirely.

5

August | Last Weekend Before 6th Grade

Another summer break is in the books. Between time spent at our family beach house and traveling around for various sports tournaments and family functions, it went by pretty fast. Now we will officially go back to school on Monday. *#NoBummerSummer*

There is a feeling when school is about to begin that is hard to mistake. First, it's in the August air. It's thick and sticky from the end of summer. If you are from the East Coast like me, you can experience three seasons all in one day. Pink cotton candy skies wake you in the morning with a warm spring hug. By afternoon, the sun is drenching every inch of your body and you actually consider moving to Alaska. Relief comes by night when the temperature drops to a cool breeze, and you can almost see autumn running towards you with a football jersey. You can for sure feel it in your stomach too, similar to fizzy soda bubbles in a bottle overflowing.

It's finally the Saturday before a new school year, a new school, a new everything. Basically, this is my last weekend of freedom, the last weekend that my story is my own. Obviously, when you are a famous Internet baby all grown up and about to start SIXTH grade, it's a stress fest. I'm still trying to figure it all out. Shouldn't I know by now, though? *#IdentityCrisis*

I spent most of mid to late summer trying to crack the code about who could have possibly smuggled me that nasty gram at orientation. The comments on the Share Faire page were here and there. Cyberbullying is taken very seriously in our house, but I managed to convince Mom to let it go for the time being. She deleted the comments as they came through but never responded, which was very unlike her! But it's best to pump the brakes and not fight with someone online. She still does not know about what happened at orientation and I intend to keep it that way.

DING… OMG, what now? The bully, who clearly had nothing better to do with their time, found my number and texted me. You guessed it:

Beware SHARE SCARE!

A knife piercing my gut, worry sliced through me - with school starting on Monday and now the text, I'm hanging over the edge by a thread. The words cut right through my last nerve, and I sprinted down the hallway to Ruby's room. Her room was neat, clean, and tastefully decorated with neutral gray colors, flowing fabrics in various shades of purple, and sparkly accents. It was very Zen like which I totally need right about now! A quote from her namesake, Ruth B. Ginsburg, was front and center. It said, "Fight for the things you care about, but do it in a way that will lead others to join you."

Ruby sat at her desk getting supplies organized for her junior year of high school. Folders flew, papers plummeted, post-it-notes stuck to the surface and index cards collected in piles. Bins of pens and pencils were sorted by type and a clipboard with more papers hung from a shelf above. This girl clearly spent a lot of her allowance at the school section of Target!

It is an important time for her too. She's looking at colleges and figuring out her lane in life. Of course, my father would love to have her go into Law and follow in his footsteps. That was his dream. My mom just wants Ruby to find her dream and follow her own path. Considering Ruby's grades, volunteering, Student Council work, and extracurricular activities, she should not have a problem. If there was a definition of model student in a dictionary, a picture of Ruby and all of her awards would be highlighted with a gold star.

The biggest question was what she wanted to do. A part of her aspires to go into public service or maybe politics. She was a true helper and advocate for people in need. However, Ruby's first love was teaching art to kids. Unfortunately, my dad has always been in her ear saying things like, "Art is a hobby, not a career." His judgments stick with her.

"What's up Marsh?" she asked as I lurked, a stage 5 stalker in the hallway.

The way she said "Marsh" calmed me, like I knew she had my back. That's her nickname for me. Now that I think of it, she is the only one who calls me Marsh.

"Nothing, I guess," as I swayed back and forth. "Just thinking about starting Weston Middle on Monday. Plus, that note nutcase from orientation apparently has my phone number now and just sent me a text taunt!"

Ruby looked concerned for the first time since the note dropped in my hand, "Are you sure you don't want Mom to call the school? This is getting a bit out of control. They could totally go Will Smith on you one day."

I know she was kidding about the last part, but my pale, crestfallen face must have told her otherwise.

Ruby looked at me with reassuring eyes, "You'll be fine. Try not to let words get to you. They are just words, you know. As for Weston, it's not as intimidating as you think. The hardest part is getting the hang of the new routine, having a locker, and switching classes which means having eight different teachers, as opposed to one. Try not to stress. As for the other stuff, you have no idea who could be targeting you. Did you tell Mom about the note, or does she just think it's a random follower doing stuff online?"

Rubbing my palm along my forehead, I turned to my big sister and said, "Mom doesn't know everything. It's best not to let that bomb explode yet. I've thought about it a lot. Based on the handwriting, it could be anyone. We can try to look up the number from the text but I'm sure it's unlisted. I know it's probably someone outside of Woodside since no one has ever called me "Share Scare" before. I just don't get why someone would do something like that. I was hoping the kids would be cool about my internet status."

Looking puzzled, Ruby's doe eyes checked in on mine, "Since when does that matter to you? They'll probably be just as nervous as you are and likely won't be overly concerned with your business. I know you are nervous, it's normal" she said, while shuffling papers into different color-coded folders.

With air quotes, I replied, "But you know, I'm kind of not normal with being Share Faire Famous and all. My close friends are cool with it and are used to the attention, but I had no idea how new kids would be about it.

That note didn't write itself and the text and chat comments did not send themselves. Now I know for sure that not all the kids will be cool about it."

"Things have always worked out for you. Being that it's out of your control how they react, you need to focus on you, not them. Do what you need to do to be comfortable. I heard someone say, you cannot choose the people around you in everyday life, but you can choose who you want to be around in your own life. Choose wisely. Be careful. Just be you."

Be Me? Easier said than done.

"Do you want to go over the map again?" she offered. I could see she was distracted, so I made my way towards the door.

"No, I think I understand the layout. Thanks Ruby."

My sister Ruby, always the helper.

Turning the corner out of Ruby's room, my ears perked up to all sorts of commotion from Annie's side of the hall.

Annie's room was the complete opposite of Ruby's room. Clothes were thrown all over the floor, medal racks and trophy shelves occupied walls, and navy-blue Penn State pennants and banners were hung as motivators. A basket in the corner held personal fitness equipment like mini dumbbells, resistance bands, and ankle weights. And there was a . . . smell.

A hoarder's paradise of empty water and Gatorade bottles were starting to overflow out of the trashcan and onto the hardwood floor. Annie was very focused on her strength and conditioning routine whenever she was not at practice. She wanted to play sports at a respected Division 1 college. Penn State is her first-choice school so laid out on her unmade bed was a Nittany Lions pillow and Penn State Athletics blanket.

Annie is going into her last year at Weston on Monday where she will be named the Co-Captain of the Field Hockey team. It's no surprise since she started playing at age four, at the height of her rant and rave phase. She is a complete monster brute, annihilating anyone in her way. My mom jokes that her stick is actually an extension of her arm and dubbed it "robo-club." She never puts it down. I think she even sleeps with it. Don't tell her I said that! *#DEAD*

I peeked my head in to see what she was up to. Clunk, Thump, Bang! Upon seeing me, she grunted, and continued fiddling with her field hockey gear. Her dirty blonde hair was up in a messy bun. Being an athlete was her priority, so she had no time for things like makeup, curling her hair, or basic hygiene. She could be twins with little orphan Annie right about now.

Clearing my throat, I tried to get her attention, "Hey Annie."

"What's going on Marshall? You never come in here," she said with sass.

Shocker!

Instead of Love, Mom should have picked Sass for her middle name! The sun filtering through the window made her hazel eyes shine, with flecks of gold flickering. While Ruby and I looked more like mom, Annie was definitely swimming in dad's gene pool. Make no mistake though, behind those beautiful eyes was a beast. You would not want to run into Annie in a dark alley. . .or anywhere really. Not one to mince words, what you see is what you get with her.

Unsure of why I was even bothering, I went on hesitantly, "Just thinking about Monday and starting Weston. It will be ok, right?"

For some reason, I really needed her reassurance that things would be just fine and that she would verbally assassinate the jerk who wrote to the semi-famous kid from the pretty famous app.

However, with great care and affection (yeah right) she retorted,

“Don’t worry. I’ll be there if you need something. Hopefully you won't though, I have enough happening with the season starting. I don't need to worry about you falling down all over the place and notes from some rando who is too much of a coward to sign their name to their threats."

“Wow, um, thanks Annie” I said dryly as I narrowed my view and crept back into the hallway. *#Bounce*

I guess I’ll have to rely on her arsenal of defense daggers only when absolutely necessary. My sister Annie, always the nurturer . . . not. It did make me feel a little better to have her in the same building, despite her charming personality. The way our campus is laid out has Elementary, Middle, and High Schools all in the same complex. So, Annie will be in the 8th Grade wing and even though Ruby attends the high school, I should be able to see her building from some of the classrooms. That helps.

My sisters seem to have ideas for their futures figured out for the most part. It is as if they dove right into the pool of life head-first. No need for flotation devices or help from lifeguards, they are able to glide smoothly through the open water with long and precise strokes. They are moving with the current, at an expeditious pace, to get to the finish line.

Then there is me, scared to test the waters on my own. I wonder if I would even try to get in the pool unless someone pushed me. Well, someone did push me into the Share Faire pool. Upon hitting the water, it feels as if I immediately sink to the bottom, fiercely kicking my way back up. Once I am at the surface, I flail for a bit before I can tread and breathe. Going upstream, I can't see the finish line. I'm not even in the race yet. Going to Weston Middle school feels like the start of the race. I just hope I can keep up and not drown on the first day. What's worse in middle school? The need for arm floaties or death by drowning? Tough call!

Without getting in too deep of what may await me in the water at Weston, I spent Saturday doing the usual stuff and taking the dog out was first on the agenda. He was dragging me out of the door before I could even get the leash on. Shedding in piles of thick multicolored fur and drooling out of the corner of his mouth, he was ready for fresh air.

Michael Jordan

My sisters begged for a dog when we were younger and promised to help raise him. Ruby even created a Google Slides presentation explaining how children thrive in environments with animals. Pointer in hand, she studiously asserted:

- Children who own dogs have higher self-esteem.
- Children who have dogs are likely to have less allergies.
- Dogs help children learn about responsibility.

Years later though, I find myself being the main kid caretaker to him since my sisters are always so busy doing something. I make sure his bowls are filled with plenty of food and water. I also take him for both leisurely and business-related walks during the day. Smarty pup knows that if he does his business, he gets rewarded with his favorite treats. My parents alternate the night shift. *#DoggieDuty*

Our fur baby is a five-year-old exuberant white and brown beagle with a hint of black tint, who pulls on the leash, smells everything within a five-mile radius, and has insane jump skills. I was only six when we met him at the shelter. My mom always thought it was hysterical for dogs to have "people names." Fido or Fluffy is much too boring. Well, first he greeted us with one outstretched paw, as if he wanted to high five the whole fam. Then he nearly jumped over the fence with his tongue hanging out to the side. We knew at that exact moment he had to be named Michael Jordan. *#GOAT*

"Are you kids seeing this? If we do not name this adorable creature after the greatest basketball player of all time, we are doing a disservice to ourselves and the entire pet naming institution!" Mom implored. Some would say she is dramatic. Others would say she speaks with flair. Either way, she's always convincing in her convictions.

I was so excited, "He looks like he's about to go old school Space Jam right about now!"

Often sporting a custom Chicago Bulls jersey made for him by one of mom's followers, this does not make our neighborhood full of Philadelphia 76ers fans so happy. In addition to jumping, he loves to chase squirrels on sight and practically dragged me up a tree last week trying to catch one. Squirrels are his weakness.

To pass more time, I played video games on the computer with friends. "Roblox" is a staple. Mom heard the screams:

"You took my pets?"

"You look SUS!"

"That wasn't a trade?"

“NOOOOOO!”

“OMG I’m out!”

A chime came through my phone, a notification from the game. I had a message.

Beware SHARE SCARE!

Ok now this is ridiculous! This person barged in on my GAME. This means war. I don't know who it is but when I find out, I’m going on a rampage. I let out a shriek of exasperation, “AHHHHHHUUUUUUGHHHH!” This is my home turf. My game world is an escape. How DARE they! This is sacred ground. *#NotCool*

“What in the world are you doing? Sounds like an episode of Stranger Things up in here!” Mom griped. I purposely stayed away from Share Faire for the time being. Since I just turned twelve, I do not have my own account, but I can search Mom’s account whenever I want. She has had a fully booked summer with different freelance writing assignments and hasn’t posted much, which I am actually grateful for. Her last posts were of my 5th Grade Graduation from Woodside.

Followers have literally watched me grow up. It was a big deal for them to see me finish elementary school. Some of them even replied with crying emojis and comments like "our little baby is all grown up." More unsolicited gifts appeared at our door. It is definitely odd for so many people to know who I am. I'm sure the kids from the other elementary schools that feed into Weston know me . . . or think they do. That includes the mystery author of the note.

I have no idea myself, so how could they?

I don't really have a "thing." Ruby's thing is art and activism. Annie's thing is clobbering anything in sight with a stick. Not one thing has defined me unless you count Share Faire. But it feels unreal sometimes. Am I worthy of the attention just because my mom was creative enough to stage me online however she wanted? Was I deserving of the recognition that followed? I struggle daily with who I am. What makes me special? What do I offer our little community except fuel for the meme fire?

As for Marshall, the person - I enjoy soccer but it's what I play, not who I am. I do well in school, but being a student is my job, it's not who I am. Who the heck am I? Well, few twelve-year-olds have it all figured out, I guess.

Being on the internet gives strangers a key to unlock perceptions and allows them entry to the safe that holds your most valued personal possessions. I can't blame my mother. She is so proud of me and my sisters that it has always been natural to share our lives with her followers online. Now that I am getting older, it appears we both have mixed feelings.

It was finally time to tell Mom the whole story. With each detail, my mom turned a different shade of red, she was almost maroon by the middle of the conversation. She pulled maniacally at strands of her hair and her head nearly spun in a full circle embodying some possessed demon.

“Who do I call? What should I do? How long has this been going on, Marshall? Why on EARTH didn’t you tell me sooner?" she wailed.

“Wow, Mom, I’m not sure, I thought maybe you’d over-react."

She did not appreciate my humor in the situation.

Even more beside herself when I showed her the crumpled-up paper from orientation day, she lunged for the phone and wanted to call the school immediately, but I grabbed her hand and begged her to back off, despite the increased presence online. I need to see how this plays out first. I have to be able to handle these things on my own. *#Mr.Independent*

Saturday night was a long night. No one slept very well. I heard my mom pacing the halls at two in the morning, burning footprint sized holes in the freshly vacuumed carpet.

My mind stirred at her reaction. The last time I saw her so spun up was when she had an argument with Mr. Bloom about Ethan Fox. Maybe we should call the Principal at Weston. I hear she's a tough one, quite the opposite of Mr. Bloom.

Mr. Bloom

Mr. Bloom is a peculiar man. He is very tall, sort of lanky in his appearance, wears suits that never quite fit right, and his hair always looks like it was styled by throwing a plugged-in toaster into a bathtub. He has no inner dialogue. He says what he thinks with little to no editing. However, he is a good person who loves all of his students and wants the absolute most successful outcome for them. He is all about learning and being the best possible version of yourself. Principal Bloom saw potential in everyone who walked through the doors of Woodside.

Mr. Bloom is the poster boy of a pre-tech consumer era. He doesn't understand why anyone would want their lives to be a viewing exhibit to strangers, especially when less than intelligent choices are involved. He knows my mother and appreciates her time volunteering on the PTO and editing our school newsletters. He did not, however, believe her public recap of Ethan's downfall was in the best taste and she took that personally.

"Hello Mrs. Hope," he said that particular day, as his 6 foot plus frame towered over my mother who is about 5 feet 5 when stretched out on a Pilates machine, at best.

"Hi, Mr. Bloom, is everything alright?" mom replied reluctantly since she could see it in his washed-out face that something was bothering him.

"Actually, I read your blog entry about Ethan Fox." His arms were crossed, and his chin lowered as he spoke. He was literally talking down to her.

Uh Oh

He continued condescendingly, "Do you think it was necessary to make a mockery of that young man's situation in the name of satire? A blog post and an animated reenactment on that Fair Cares Sharing app thing-a-ma-jig. Wasn't that a bit much? True journalism does not pass judgment, Mrs. Hope."

Saltier than the ocean, mom spat back, "That young man created his situation on his own and is old enough to know better. My blog is not for everyone, Mr. Bloom. If you do not like what you are reading on my page or seeing on the app, then you have the option to stop and look elsewhere. By the way, it's called Share Faire. You should think about investing some time getting acquainted with it, since most of your upper grade students use it. Stay connected and have a nice day." *#Boom*

My mom never viewed her involvement with Share Faire or being an internet blogger as being a lesser career choice. She did her time in stuffy Corporate America and was able to stay home and still provide income by doing something she loved.

She certainly could never have imagined what it would be like for me once I grew out of my Justice Marshall phase. At the height of it all, she was on a tiered pay plan with Share Faire and supplemented our household income with freelance writing and product promotion. I don't necessarily think she "used" me for fame although many have accused her of that. I think she was just doing what most moms do - take photos and post them online. She had no way of knowing the detonation of hype that would come along with it.

6

August | Sunday Before School Panic

Despite being sleep deprived my mom did not disappoint this morning. We have a tradition in our family that we have a huge breakfast on the Sunday before school starts. Since our schedules will be all over the place, it's rare when we can eat together in the morning, so it's an elaborate affair. The smell of pancakes caked the air. Sizzling sausage and bacon nearly set off the smoke alarm. Fruit dipped in Nutella was a decadent treat and Dad makes a deliciously tangy juice that we often consume by the gallon. I think it's orange and papaya mixed with a dash of fairy dust and happiness!

While planning family gatherings, my mom loves a theme and always gets special plates and decorations to add pizazz. She does the same for our birthdays. The nook in our kitchen is completely transformed. It's always so exciting to come downstairs on our special day and see paper lanterns, streamers, signs, in whatever theme she chose.

Today, for our annual back to school breakfast, everything was decorated with "sunshine." Sunny plates, bright yellow balloons, and swirly decorations in the bold hue dangled from the windows. A banner that said, "Always find the bright side of things" draped across the French doors. The emoji wearing sunglasses was in the middle. A gift was placed on each of our seats around the table- that same emoji in stress ball form. I guess that was the lesson for this year. With all of the changes coming, we need to find the bright side.

#TheSunWillComeOutTomorrow

After breakfast, we spent most of the day together doing fun stuff at the nearby park. It is within walking distance of our house, and it boasts tennis courts, sports fields, playground equipment, and this spectacular outdoor amphitheater where our town holds concerts and plays over the summer. It's historic with architecturally curved arches and chiseled design patterns that have been preserved over hundreds of years. At night, twinkling lights within white sphere bulbs are strung across the high-beamed framework. The illuminated stage gives character and charm to the park.

We brought Michael, who definitely kept us on our toes. He tried to smell a toddler, eat bird doodie, and lick another dog's tail. Thankfully, no squirrel sightings.

Ruby yelled from across the park, "Annie, can you help me with Michael Jordan? He's trying to become a member of that duck family over there but they're rejecting him ruthlessly." *#Quackitude*

In the distance park goers could see Ruby hanging onto the dog's leash for dear life, struggling to hold him back from a group of bitter ducks. The mama duck must have thought he was trying to snack on her babies because she was in full protective mode. Michael is barking, Mama Duck is hissing, Baby Ducks are shaking and quaking, all while Ruby is flustered and absolutely freaking out. It's not even a scene at this point, it's a domestic duck vs. dog disturbance!

Too engrossed in practicing her field hockey shooting skills, Annie could not properly reply. So a series of strangled sounds came out of her mouth. Finally, she looked up and snidely asked, "Zone Defense or Man to Man? Are the ducks Blocking or Charging?"

Not amused, Ruby demanded, "What does that even mean, Annie?" Chaos was still ensuing in the background.

Suppressing a chuckle, she signaled to me, then clearly bellowed, "Marshall can do it."

Of course!

Ruby helped me keep him in line. We fit the “bill!” Once the animal conflict was properly resolved and settled out of court, we absorbed the beauty of the park. Butterfly wings fluttering about was a beautiful display. The sun roasted us from head to toe. Hearing the laughter and excited cries of children playing on swings and slides made us smile. Finally, the smell of flowers from the nearby garden tickled our noses. We could practically taste the roses. It was an awesome gift from nature. A little while later, Ruby soaked up some rays while I worked out some worries on the field.

Like Annie, I brought my sports bag. Footwork drills and dribbling my soccer ball along the sidelines, I ran. Up and down the field and back again, I ran. Then I ran some more, faster, and faster. I ran to flee the new school year. I ran to elude the cyber bully. I ran to find myself. The wind hit my back and I was gone. Running more rapidly than I could ever remember, I started to panic. I get anxious a lot, but I have never had a full-on panic attack . . . until now.

Struggling to breathe, I dropped to my knees. My limbs trembled while I gulped for air. Seconds away from throwing up, Ruby rushed to my aid. As hard as I tried, I could not get the orientation bully out of my head. How did that person get my phone number? GASP How on Earth did they get in my game? GASP I'm still 100 percent peeved about that. It was all too much to think about on the day before school. Can't breathe, GASP, dark skies, GASP, eyes heavy. Short of breath and my heart racing, I managed to sip the water Ruby held out for me.

She stroked my hand, "You're ok Marsh. Just take small sips." She was a calming force, but I could see the concern flashing in neon yellow all over her face. This was bad.

Being on the app never really impacted my sisters one way or another. I guess they got some occasional comments about their Share Faire famous brother. They couldn't avoid it entirely. My mom would post Ruby's art or brag about her report cards. She would sometimes make videos that highlighted Annie's talents on the field. People watched and responded on a regular basis.

But for some reason, my videos were way more popular. The girls were never jealous though. Ruby was proud and Annie basically couldn't care less. Their friends thought it was cute that I was "Justice Marshall" but nothing about Share Faire interfered with their lives. That wasn't the case for me. Whether I was playing soccer, playing games, or just playing around, people knew who I was.

I finally calmed down and was able to compose myself enough to make it back home. We tiptoed across the street and also around what happened today. I was embarrassed and had enough to do in order to get ready for school tomorrow. Ain't nobody got time for this! A long hot shower will do the trick.

Ruby filled in Mom on the events of the afternoon while I savored the steamy solitude of the shower. I washed the dirt from my skin and the memory of the panic attack from my brain. This is not who I am . . . or maybe it is. I really need to figure my crap out.

I welcomed the pitter patter of the rain outside as I settled into my bed. The soothing drops tapped the window rhythmically and nature's soundtrack nearly put me to sleep. I hoped I would have some classes with my friends. I really needed Caden by my side. I drifted in and out of a hazy fog with a memory of our one and only fight as best friends.

Caden

In third grade during Woodside's yearly "Field Day" we were on different teams. The competition was wicked, and everyone wanted their team to win the "Nine Juan Juan

Taco Truck" lunch reward. They had the best Mex Munch in town and the truck has a towering sombrero on the roof! Aside from tasty tacos, photo ops near the truck would be enough reason to want victory.

The matches were pretty even up until the last event which was Battle Beam. Basically two students stood on a balance beam and tried to knock each other off of the beam with foam paddles. It came down to me and Caden. I am not overly competitive like Annie, but I don't want to lose either. Both Caden and I are pretty strong from all of our sports training, and it was an epic contest.

The violent impact of the paddle - thwack, smack, whack - combined with the excitement from the crowd, made for a collision course of taco envy!

In the end, I was able to overpower and hurl him off the beam. As a result, my team was treated to a wide array of tacos in Woodside's outdoor classroom. *#TacoBoutAWin*

Caden didn't talk to me for a week. I totes understand, a food truck is his mother ship, and he had the appetite of a starved alien. Still, I was mad that he was mad! But like most male conflicts in school, it eventually blew over. One person needs to decide that enough is enough. When I showed up at Caden's door with his favorite fast food BBQ Cheeseburger and chili fries, it was hard for him to stay upset. *#NoFoodFight*

Startled by thunder and no longer asleep, thoughts of my classmates filled my head as I tossed and turned to find the right position… Are they this nervous? Maybe. Caden? Doubt it. He does not seem to ever get tense or uneasy about anything. Caden tends to skate by on a rink of his good looks and charisma. He's right on the cut off for Hall 2 with a last name that starts with "L." It sure would be nice to have him there.

Still reeling from the panic attack, I figured it would be a good time for a self-pep talk! I mean, I am that Justice

Marshall kid from Share Faire. That has to give me some clout, right? And just like that, finally found the sleep zone.

7

August | First Day of 6th Grade

My alarm didn't even have a chance to go off. I was jolted awake by the madness of the morning. Clinks of glassware and creaking cabinet doors were heard throughout the kitchen. The drip of the coffee pot and sweet aroma of muffins were a welcome hug on my first day, adding a layer of comfort in the chaos. Mom was gathering everyone's things and making sure we had what we needed. Backpacks, paperwork, and sport bottles cluttered the countertops. Mom's attempt to go stealth mode was unsuccessful. We totally watched her tuck good luck notes into our bags in plain view. She's next level thoughtful.

Ruby is the first to leave.

"Mom," she whispered tenderly. "I am fully able and willing to take the bus. I promise it will be fine."

She recited this line every year on the first day of school and every year the response was the same. Mom put her hands on Ruby's shoulders with affection,

"Sweetie Pie, I know you are capable, but we love doing it for you. Someday you will drive yourself. Let us have you while we can."

In fact, mom's words were never timelier. Ruby is sixteen which means she will be driving this year! *#GetOffTheRoads*

We have never taken the bus in all of our years of school other than for field trips. Dad would drop off Ruby on his way into the office or my mom would drive her if he had an early meeting. Mom always drove Annie and me. It was one less thing she had to worry about. Getting to school safely every day meant something to her.

I know my mom had a hard time in school and was bullied. It started on the bus. Here's a simple middle school equation in the subject of hormonal girls:

An awkward phase + a misunderstanding = irrational emotion. My mom was on the receiving end of some horrific irrational emotion.

She rarely talks about it, but I know it hurts her tender heart. *#BullyingSucks*

A blur of activity marked the morning. Pulling my sweatshirt over my head and grabbing my shoes, next thing I knew, we were heading out the door in a hurry. I gave Michael a squeeze goodbye and rushed to the car. Boink! Annie nearly knocked me over with all of her stuff. Swinging her backpack over her shoulder, her hands were full of field hockey gear and I'm quite sure her spikes nearly stabbed me.

As usual, I would get no remorse from her. With my hands on my hips and a scowled expression on my face, I waited patiently for an apology that never came. She only responded with an annoyed, “What?” All I could muster in return was an irritated, “Seriously?”

I clutched and kneaded my stress ball during the entire ten-minute ride to school. Approaching the congested drop off circle at Weston, I was actually okay. I rationalized an internal coping strategy. I already knew a lot of kids between school and soccer. Plus, Annie’s friends always treated me like their little brother (Ruby’s friends did too). This will be fine. I can't let three words ruin my whole first day!

As predicted, I was in Hall 2. I was psyched because I could see Caden made the cut and also had homeroom in Hall 2. Our lockers were pretty close together.

His high five hung midair and ready to rock, Caden approached me with zeal, “Dude! Marshall! What’s up?

Have you seen all of these girls running around? Everyone grew up over the summer, even since orientation. Some things are, um, new. How are we supposed to concentrate?" he said with a wicked glint in his turquoise tinted eye. We are at the age where we are beginning to notice things.

The girls were already starting to spot Caden, a collection of beating organs lining up to see which one he'd break first. At this point, I was his "Wing Man" - a Share Faire Famous Wing Man. I wasn't really into girls the way other boys my age were. I mean, I see them, I like them, but I'd rather play sports than play emotional games with tween girls. I was happy living in the friend zone. It's safe there.

It's hard not to get affected when all eyes are burning a crater into your brain. I've been used to this my whole life. An innocent smile normally was enough to hold people off. Some people simply say, "hi or hey." Interest and volume started to build into a preteen explosion of hype. Ding Ping

Ring - phones were singing a gossipy song nonstop before they were put away. The clicking of fingers dancing across device screens was hard to ignore.

There were kids who got extremely animated and yelled, "OMG it's the Share Faire Kid" or "Yo Justice Marshall." There may have been some shrieking and gawking in the crowded hallway. Others, though, were in their own world and walked or stumbled unaware. I could do this. No sign of anyone suspicious. I'm looking on the bright side.

My classes all seemed to be manageable. I overheard conversations and felt the glaring eyes of my classmates though. One girl questioned within ear shot, "I wonder if he will make a video with us." Another chimed in saying, "Try to get a picture of him." *#OnTheSly*

There was a strict no phone rule at Weston. They were to be stored in lockers at all times, the sharp metal vibrated to the beat of students stowing away their devices. But tweens found sneaky ways to get around it. Kids often made videos in the halls, behind the building, or even in bathrooms. The girl in question managed to take my photo like a slimy paparazzi and later posted it to the tune of a thousand likes and hundreds of new followers. She hash tagged the pic with "*#AllRiseJusticeMarshallAtWeston.*"

But I was at school to learn, not to give autographs. My dad is a broken record on the importance of working hard and getting good grades. A proper education was first and foremost. My mom was even keel. She kept the demand lower. She just wanted us to try our best and, if needed, we would figure out a solution if we did not understand a task. My parents canceled each other out pretty well.

The morning was worse than getting shot with nerf pellets. Trying to follow a schedule and locate each classroom in a new building took military grade timing. Changing classes with precision and agility, finding camouflaged lockers, and then attempting to open the locker, all before the bell exploded, err - rang, was a boot camp in middle school survival. Sixth Grade Soldiers were faltering:

"My locker won't open."

"Where is room 202B?"

"I want to go hooooommmme!"

A little dazed and dizzy, I thought it was just from the Sixth Grade Drill Sergeants, um teachers, zapping my energy but it was actually lunchtime. Since each grade eats lunch all together, I already planned to eat with Caden and some of our soccer friends.

I shoved my books inside the narrow locker and reached for my lunch. A leggy girl with long straight blonde hair was headed straight toward me. She looked like she knew her way around a mall. Lip gloss poppin' and outfit stylin', I admit that she was good looking. Maybe she knew me from Share Faire. Maybe she even had a crush on me. I do not know her. She must have come from one of the other feeder schools. Upon further review though, she kind of looked familiar, one of the girls who was eyeing me up in a weird way at orientation. She oozed anger out of her flawless pores and is on some sort of mission. Sapphire blue eyes pierced my face like laser beams.

Is it hot in here?

Was I sweating?

Ella

She marched up and through gritted teeth said, "I know you. You are that Share SCARE kid."

I took a couple of steps back and said, "What? You mean Share Faire?"

"No, I said Share SCARE, Meme Boy. You seem to have grown into your head."

She moved closer to me and then the lightbulb went off in my head.

IT's HER! SHE wrote the note. SHE posted the comment on Share Faire. SHE interrupted my game. SHE sent the text. Never in my life did I want to strangle a Barbie Doll.

I was so mad I was about to liquify from fury and sweat, ultimately evaporating directly into the Earth.

Shocked and bothered, I did not hesitate to ask, “What’s your problem?”

Her face tightened and her mouth opened, and I expected venom would shoot out at any second.

Oh no.

“Beware SHARE SCARE. Don't get any idea that you will be the most popular kid in sixth grade just because you are on the Internet. My friends and I are queens. We are the Crown Crowd, we ruled our school, and this year will be no different. We know what we want and how to get it. Got it?”

I honestly did not know what to say to that, so like any boy my age I barked,

“Get a life."

She whipped around so fast.

What have I done?

“You’ll see what kind of life I have, and what I can do to yours! Try not to fall down in the meantime."

Ugh Harsh!

The cranky girl in her fancy boots stomped aggressively down the hall. *#TheseBootsAreMadeforStompin*

By the time I got to lunch I felt like I went 10 rounds with Rocky. The color drained from my face, and I was wiped.

It’s a GIRL. A freaking GIRL. Warning ME about popularity. What in the world . . .

Mouths hit the table as I told the guys at lunch how she was responsible for practically ruining my summer. Sam jumped from his chair and shouted, “Oh, sounds like you met the lovely Ella Price!” Another kid from across the way added, “She’s hot but a bit of a Queen Bee . . . and I’m not talking about the Bees that Buzz."

“Who is she?” we asked.

“She’s from Wells Elementary. She and a group of four girls basically ran Wells. They set the trends, the tone, and decided who was in and what wasn't. I think the power went to their heads. They call themselves the Crown Crowd and go around adjusting their fictitious crowns all day.”

“How is that even allowed to happen?” Caden was puzzled but he still managed to ask his question while simultaneously stuffing his face with pizza, a luxury food choice in middle school.

Sam continued, “Well, her mom is well known in the community. She is the VP of a Graphic Design firm, so she works with a lot of local businesses and organizations. All of Ella’s projects were professionally done. Her dad is a big wig that works in the city. They have stupid money, the kind of cash you could buy a unicorn with if you had the right connections, which they do. Their house is practically a museum. Guess it’s called privilege." *#UnicornMoney*

Hmm. By no means were any of us in our neighborhood gazillionaires but we were all well taken care of and lived in nice houses. No Unicorns in sight. Two story, center hall colonials with brick fronts, custom windows, and velvety jade green yards were common but nothing resembling a museum.

Ella Price sure had it out for me and any fame or recognition that I had. She felt threatened and usually when people feel threatened, they attack. I prepared myself for a situation like this when I talked to my sister over the weekend. Her words echoed in my head, "it's out of your control how people react. You need to focus on yourself."

This day was starting to test my ability to find the bright side. Much to my dismay, my last two classes after lunch are Math and Social Studies. I don't love math but I'm decent at it. I really am into Social Studies since we cover a lot about different types of people, history, geography and culture. Ruby always enjoyed learning about social studies, so I do too by association.

A strong whiff of perfume attacked my nose. Yup, Ella Price. Here. In my Social Studies class. She grimaced at me when she walked in and then motioned to a girl who was equally dolled up and swanky. Another member of the Crown Crowd, I assumed.

Being all extra, they squealed shrilly, “yes queen," adjusted a fake crown on the top of their heads, and then scoffed my way. I rolled my eyes so far in the back of my head I practically saw my brain.

I took my seat and glanced around the room for some familiar faces. There were a few including Mollie Banks.

Mollie

I always liked Mollie. She’s been with us at Woodside from the start. She’s really cute in an understated way - quiet - but very smart. Her wavy reddish-brown hair changes tone with the weather and her emerald, green eyes are wide, as if she's always learning and discovering new things. Mollie is preppy in the way she dressed but it was real to who she was, not like she was playing the part of the gifted kid in a school play. She really did shop at Gap and Old Navy because that is what she felt comfortable in.

Mollie doesn't need glitter and sequins to shine, she gleams on her own. She's real and in middle school, real is hard to find. Side note, Caden always blushes when Mollie is around, which is weird since girls normally blush over him. *#Flipped*

Mollie lives in the townhome development that backs up to our neighborhood. Sometimes she comes over to visit Michael when he plays with his bones outside. She doesn't have a large group of friends, but people think highly of her and admire how advanced she is with her studies. She would certainly be a candidate for "Most Likely to Succeed" in a school yearbook. She waved and I gave her a friendly grin. Ella noticed this. I could see the fire in her eyes. *#NewTarget.*

"Hey Red, how do you know Scary?" she called from the back of the room.

Mollie didn't really know how to respond. She adjusted the bottom of her fitted periwinkle collared shirt against her tan chino pants, and simply asked, "Excuse me?" She did not squirm in her chair or let Ella know just how anxious the whole exchange made her.

There was no time to continue since the teacher hurried in and immediately began to talk incessantly about Egyptian culture. We did not even get a chance to take out our textbooks. We took notes on pyramids, hieroglyphics, and pharaohs. So much for easing us into the first day. Thanks, Teach.

Things at Wells Elementary are certainly different from our home school Woodside. Everyone was friends there. There weren't any cliques, we all just clicked and coexisted.

It was just easy. I was starting to get the impression that this year at Weston would be anything but easy.

8

6th Grade Transitions into Fall

We pretty much live in my mom's midsize SUV. It's in constant disarray with a collection of empty coffee cups littered with written thoughts tossed in. In our family, this vehicle is known as "Laura's Hot Mess Express" for obvious reasons. However, she calls it Tom Hanks. Why? As she told the car dealer the day it was purchased, "Because you can always count on Tom Hanks, and I want a car as reliable in function as Tom is in making great films." Exasperated, the dealer shook his head and handed her the keys. My mom has that effect on strangers.

In addition to being eccentric, she is very visual. The action of writing, pen to paper, is preferred over making lists on her phone. This time, however, she did not toss them into the wind. She collected the doodles for whenever the moment struck. Sometimes the car lines were long, so while she waited for us to come out, she took those opportunities to compile ideas for articles.

An observer to her core, she once wrote about how kids walk when leaving school. Not a topic that typically sets the publishing world ablaze, but she made it work. Some run to their cars with arms flailing like overzealous Kindergartners while others simply zombie stroll. The kids who linger and socialize are normally slow, while the kids who are rushing to a practice tend to zip. There was almost always a distracted kid looking down at his or her phone, presumably scrolling through Share Faire, who nearly tucked and rolled to their bus from not watching where they were going. A very simple premise turned into a post that was shared among many. She had the ability to take the dry and mundane and build it into a word playhouse furnished with imagery and prose. *#WordSmith*

I plopped in the car, threw my backpack into the backseat and furiously filled my mom in on the events of my first day. Annie's field hockey practice got canceled, so she was actually listening too. When I got to the part about Ella Price being my not-so-secret admirer, I could see my mom's blood start to boil. Talking wildly with my hands and amplified expressions made me look like one of those massive floaty guys outside of a gas station car wash. I was on point with the play by play.

"Then she basically told me she would destroy my life!" I may have slightly exaggerated that part but, really, normal people don't go around threatening people on the first day of school!

"She even went after sweet Mollie!" I added.

“Do you want me to call the school?" Mom asked with a growl of anger that gurgled in her voice.

“No, mom. I’ve got this," I assured her.

My mother had no patience for bullies, especially considering her past and having to deal with online trolls who always had an opinion about what she posted on Share Faire. People can be ridiculously mean. Someone actually commented that my oversized head as a baby was due to a frontal lobe brain tumor. #*Wrong*

OK, calm down Doctor Google!

Another said they wanted to punt me across Lincoln Financial Field. I mean, what? Who hurt you? Before having that person blocked permanently from her account, she gave them a piece of her mind. Her written words were sharp, and her laptop was the sword. Cross a line and you will pay.

Even more surprising was Annie’s reaction to my Ella story. She normally does not pay attention to anything that concerns me, but this time was different. Her body flexed, hands balled into fists, and her face was stone.

"She said WHAT to you? Are you kidding me? Show me who she is so I can shove my field hockey stick up her.."

"ANNIE!" yelled mom, before she had a chance to finish.

Cackles filled the car and before long we were all hunched over in our seats, out of breath in hysterics.

The first few weeks of school went by at warp speed. Between my classes, recreation league soccer, gaming nights, and fighting off taunts from Ella and Crown Crowd, there was not a lot of time for much else. They took to calling me "Lollipop." I guess it was another swipe at the big-headed baby chapter of my story. Lollipop Lollipop, a song from the golden oldies would play on their phones after school as I walked to the car, as if it was my assigned anthem. They'd also drop lollipops in huge piles by my locker, but if I am being honest, I don't actually mind that part. Neither does Caden.

Their efforts were elaborate, but I'm keeping things together. My grades are fine and I'm on track for the honor roll, which makes Professor Preachy Pants happy. Did I mention my dad is as fun as a box of dictionaries?

Each day was the same structure but vastly different in how it unfolded. Some days were better than others. The days where people fist-bumped me just for being that "Share Faire kid" were easy. The days when Ella and her Crown Crowd made appearances were admittedly harder but not nearly as hard as it was for Mollie. Ella got wind that Mollie lived in a townhouse and labeled her "poor little Mollie." She was relentless.

First of all, Mollie's family is not poor. Her mother is a stay-at-home mom, and her dad is a Financial Advisor. They lived modestly by choice, not out of need. Mollie's mom assumed the role of Homeroom Mom for five straight years at Woodside, so she was always super involved in school events. Staying home allowed her to be there for Mollie whenever she wanted.

Living in their townhome also allowed them to buy a rustic mountain house in the Poconos. They love their weekend getaways at the shabby chic cabin, spent biking the trails and boating on the serene lake. Mollie is an only child and does not want anything, but at the same time, is not spoiled. Everything she has is earned. She excels in academics and plays the cello. She pretty much swept our 5th Grade awards ceremony and was the District Math League Champion. There is nothing poor about Mollie Banks. She was rich in ways I was just beginning to notice. *#EyesOpen*

The first official day of Fall hit me in the face with a pinch of cinnamon. I love the pumpkin spice world domination that happens every September (so does mom) and we are obsessed with the smell of burnt leaves in the crisp chilled air. With the change in season comes a lot of different clubs and activity opportunities for the school.

An email was distributed this morning listing all of the club options, which included: sports, languages, cooking, art, music, and more. Students are able to select two clubs. Of course, I'll play 6th grade soccer, that was a given. I wracked my brain to come up with one more. I scanned the list backwards and forwards. The record skipped in my head to the beat of Dad drumming the importance of being a well-rounded individual. So the Student Council grade level clubs jumped out at me. There will even be an election! Just as Ruby did years ago, I'll run for something and represent my grade.

My thoughts were like scrambled eggs in my head. The sizzle was broken up by someone yelling from across the room, "Hey Justice Marshall, you'd be a shoe in for President. Everyone knows you. You RULE. Just get your mom's Share Faire followers on board." I chuckled. He had a point. *#Totes*

As the weeks went on at Weston Middle, aside from the Crown Crowd, making friends was not so hard. All of the worries that I had at the beginning of the year seemed pointless now. Being Share Faire famous helped for sure. I knew I had to weed out the bad seeds but overall, everyone was pretty cool. I could absolutely run in the election and use my mom's platform for votes.

That would not necessarily be the right thing to do. Easy? Yes. Right? Not exactly. Plus, I was becoming more unsettled about that part of my life anyway.

(Bloom's Basics Number 1 - Always be Honest).

Mr. Bloom's questions from months ago still lingered in my mind:

"What would you do?"

"If given the chance, would you take the easy way out? Or would you do the right thing?"

If I am doing this, I will do it the right way, not take the easy way. After all, my future depends on it.

Bubbly banter floated through the hallways about the email. What kid would choose which club is the hot topic of the morning. A meeting after school will be held later in the week for anyone interested in running for Student Council. I'm in! Why not, right?

On Friday, a bunch of 6th graders were already elbow to elbow and stumping for votes at the meeting when I rolled in. They were signing the sheet for the position that interested them the most. The positions available were President, Vice President, Corresponding Secretary, Recording Secretary, and Treasurer.

The President and Vice President worked together to determine how to best meet the needs of the students. This was done by planning events like information forums, picnics, or pep rallies. The Treasurer managed the sixth-grade funds to finance each special outing. Ruby was always the Recording Secretary. She took the meeting notes and chronicled all of the happenings at the school. She would then give the information to the Corresponding Secretary who was responsible for communicating it to the students. Ruby liked to make an impact behind the scenes. Like the Director of a Play, she kept the show running but allowed others to be seen center stage.

Honestly, the rough and tumble boy in me did not want a title that had the word "Secretary" in it. It sounded too much like a girl's job. Having two sisters, I need to be more sensitive to feminism. I instantly felt like a bad brother. Not to mention, Ruth Bader Ginsburg was likely rolling in her grave at that thought. *#NotoriousRBG*

I could run for Treasurer but then again, I hate math. That left the President or Vice President positions to pick from. I was already a front and center kind of kid. The words of my classmate echoed in my head, "You'd be a shoe in for President. Everyone knows you." I took a breath, signed my name on the sheet for President and turned on my heels to leave. Who was behind me, also waiting to sign up for President? If the perfume stinks . . . You guessed it, Ella Price.

Before she could direct her poison towards me, we both noticed that Mollie Banks was ambitiously coming towards the President sign-up sheet. Her brown loafers tapped the floor in a staccato tempo as she asserted herself into the mix. Oh boy, this was not going to be easy at all. With Ella and the Crown Crowd and Mollie and her academic superiority, I was not a shoe in, I was the underdog.

"What do you think you are doing? Poor Mollie, you won't stand a chance against me. Wouldn't you be more comfortable in the background? May I suggest, Treasurer? You could finally see what money looks like up close. Impoverished children should be seen and not heard" Ella spewed.

Pushing buttons left and right, she then came at me, exposing self-doubts previously kept hidden away - "And YOU? Share SCARE, really? What are you going to do, have Mommy get votes for you?"

GEEZ, how does she just worm her way inside my head, set up camp, and forward all her mail there? She fixed her imaginary crown and aimed her crystal blue eyes right into my spirit.

Words penetrating, she continued her opinionated assault, "Look, Mr. Lollipop. For someone with such an enormous head, your brain is miniscule. Drop out now while you can. No one cares about a kid who peaked while in diapers!"

Not one to wake up and choose violence, anger consumed me in a way that felt unnatural. I wanted to take the high road, but I couldn't.

Just as I was about to channel my inner Annie and unleash savagery and insult on her, Mollie interrupted and said with poise, “It’s an open election. We have as much of a right to run as you do. May the best person for the job win." *#HighClass*

Jaws dropped! Who is Regal now?

Mollie amazed me. How could she be so calm and composed? How could she not want to yell and scream? Honestly, how could she not want to slap Ella in her smug face? That was one of the more admirable things about Mollie. Not only was she smart but humble as well. She knew she was the smartest person in the room but never made you feel less than because of it. She’s a good person and I wasn’t sure how I had a shot. In a fair fight, she’d win by a landslide.

But this was Middle School and there was no such thing as a fair fight. Ella’s strategy would surely be to round up the Crown Crowd and promise popularity and refuge from her hostility to all who supported her. She would absolutely prey on people’s insecurities and, let’s face it; most kids are insecure at our age. I could not let that happen.

#LifeIsNotAlwaysFair

9

September, Campaign and Crush Season Begin

Today is unofficially Groundhog Day. Write a bad campaign idea on a piece of paper, crumple said paper, throw it across the room, and repeat! Good ideas for my campaign were hard to come by. How could I stop the Crown Crowd? How could I run against Mollie but also protect her from Ella at the same time? How could I win this election without using my Share Faire fame? One post and this would be over. So many questions and no answers.

Michael scampered into my room and started to whimper. He wanted to take a walk. As usual, my sisters were missing in action when it came to pup parenting. I need a break from my over-thinking anyway. My head was ready to burst, so I leashed him up and we roamed the neighborhood. Bushels of apples, mums, hay bales, and scarecrows decorated the street. More evidence of Fall's arrival were tons of leathery acorn shells strewn across the sidewalk. Michael tried to make several squirrel friends along the way. They were not receptive. *#MeanSquirrels*.

I recognized the path that connects Mollie's neighborhood to mine. I often walked Michael around the townhomes for a change of scenery. With three levels, dramatic front entryways, and professionally manicured common areas, the townhouses were a very desirable place to live, contrary to Ella's skewed views. Losing my footing, Michael pulled me down the street and there was Mollie, sitting on her front steps scribbling frantically in a notebook. In the bright daylight, it was easier to see the pale freckles scattered around her nose and arms. Her hair now looked auburn as the haze of summer turned into a pure blue hue of Autumn. Her curls were pulled up in a high ponytail held with a gray and white polka dot scrunchie. My stomach fluttered, and I felt odd upon seeing her.

What was that all about?

"Hey Mollie," I called out, trying to keep the belly butterflies at bay.

"Oh. Hi, Marshall."

Her voice then changed to baby talk, "And hewwo dere Mikey Wikey."

She loves dogs and happily came up to pet him. He jumped up to her eye level and licked her bottom lip like it was water ice on a balmy beach day. After a momentary pause in the love fest, he tackled Mollie again and I yanked him back, spinning in a circle that trapped all three of us in the leash. He growled with jealousy as we giggled and wiggled and untangled ourselves back to freedom.

"Are you planning out your campaign?" I asked with a lump in my throat.

"I am trying to, but I honestly can't find an angle that will give me an advantage to win. You have the popular vote. Ella and her crew have the intimidation and bribery vote. I can get the Honor Society vote but that's a very small audience," she explained while scratching her head with a pencil.

We spent the next twenty minutes talking, laughing, and brainstorming together. It suddenly hit me like a ton of bricks. I knew what to do.

"Hey Mollie, what do you think about teaming up and running as Co-Presidents?"

Surprised and eager, she enthusiastically asked, "Wait, can we DO that?"

"I think so. When my sister was on the Student Council in 7th grade there were Co-Vice Presidents so I'm sure they would allow Co-Presidents. We can ask the advisor on Monday."

"Yes!" Mollie exclaimed.

On Monday, word got around the Sixth Grade Wing that the Student Council Club Advisor approved our request to run as Co-Presidents. Mollie is coming over after school and we are going to lay the groundwork for our campaign. As you can imagine, Ella and the Crown Crowd are royally ticked to hear about my alliance with Mollie:

"Just who do they think they are? Meghan and Harry? You saw what Queen Elizabeth and the Monarchy did to THEM . . . wait for me, you haven't seen anything yet!" *#Ousted*

Their wrath was felt throughout the halls. Turbulent volcanic tantrums flooded the corridors. I followed Mollie's lead and didn't react, even though I often wanted to take Annie up on her offer to beat Ella with a field hockey stick.

I could not help but wonder though, how did Mollie's feelings not get hurt? Ella was nasty to her every chance she got. I tried not to let it get to me. As a boy, it was different, I guess. Mean Girls is not just a movie, it's a real thing and you need a thick skin to handle it, especially in middle school. I know how much my mom is still affected all of these years later. Would that happen to Mollie?

More Flutters. What is happening?

I worried about it for a hot second, but it was time to leave. I grabbed my backpack and met up with Mollie by her locker. She was smiling with flushed cheeks but then her expression quickly changed.

Do I stink?

No. Ella was on her way over and stormed through a group of innocent bystanders to get to us.

"Do you actually think teaming up will help you? Think again!" her voice amped up.

She feverishly fixed her fake crown and all of a sudden, there was a flash. It was Annie bolting towards the gym for field hockey practice. She watched our exchange happening with Ella and she was in NO MOOD. Annie wedged her way in between us and so it began . . .

"Hey, Princess," Annie yelled.

"I think you mean Queen," Ella replied without missing a beat.

This girl really had no fear.

"I heard you like to bully people. Well, I'm in 8th grade. You better check yourself before you wreck yourself. If you don't, so help me, I will knock that ridiculous fake crown off of your head with my stick so fast you won't know what hit you. I suggest you find your glass slipper, hop in your pumpkin coach, and get out of here NOW!" *#Boss*

A small group had gathered and gasped. It was a spectacle!

All Ella could do was let out an unfazed laugh and say "whatever."

Before I could move a muscle, Annie pounced toward her when a voice cried out. UH OH! Principal Taylor. Dressed in a tailored tan suit, pointy heels, and holding a walkie, she had a much more forceful presence as an administrator than Mr. Bloom.

“Miss Hope, if you plan to use that stick ever again on a field, I advise that you get to your practice, or I will write you up for disobedience. Everyone else. Go home.”

Annie grumbled something I couldn’t quite understand and left for practice but not before giving Ella the evil eye and me a sly smile. Annie had my back! *#MiddleSisBodyguard*

Mollie had a note to let my mother pick her up from school. Mom waited in the pick-up circle, and we hopped in the car, frantic to tell our tale. She couldn't believe what Annie had done but deep down I think she was secretly proud. Ragey Robo-club to the rescue!

10

Late September | M&M

Greeting us upon arrival at the house was the aroma of hot cocoa and warm gooey cookies. I didn't even take my first sip when I heard the doorknob rattling. Caden is here. Of course, he is. He sensed it whenever we had snacks, especially sweets. It's like he has nose radar or something. He's been shamelessly eating our food for years. Plus, I think he has a little thing for Mollie, but he would never admit it. I couldn't blame him. The jock drawn to the bookworm is a great plot line for a television show but in middle school, images were to be protected and feelings were guarded.

“What’s up Political People," he harmonized as he danced his way into the kitchen.

Upon seeing Mollie, he pulled back the act, and was bashful, of all things!

Caden’s, “Hey Mollie," came out about two octaves higher than his normal voice and he tripped over his own shoes while getting into the chair. It screeched across the kitchen floor, and we all covered our ears in protest.

Devouring the cookies was easy. Coming up with ideas was another thing. We threw thoughts around for a theme but nothing stuck. Caden’s “Beauty and the Beast” campaign slogan suggestion was met with a collective thud and furthermore, a confused look from Mollie. It must have intrigued her though since her pale complexion turned pink in an instant. Although I’m offended at being referred to as a hairy horror, the overall point just validated what I knew all along, Caden liked Mollie. This stings but I wasn't really sure why or how. Mollie was my running mate, nothing more. Caden always saw her differently. It wasn't a secret. So why do I still feel off balance?

Thank goodness mom came in and halted my emotional introspective. She was thrilled about the election and had ideas for us if we needed them. She had artistry, as evidenced by her writing. Although I wanted to do this on my own, it would not hurt to get her input. I was pretty clear though when I told her that I did NOT want to include Share Faire in any way!

"Mom, promise you won't post any of this on Share Faire, OK?" I pleaded.

"Marshall, I said I wouldn't, but I really don't understand. My followers are talented folks. They may have some useful tips," she offered.

"I know, but I want to do this on my own, my way. You can help but it stays within these walls."

(Bloom's Basics #2 - Be True to Yourself)

The first order of business was to come up with a campaign mission list. What did we want to accomplish as Co-Presidents? How would we capture everyone's attention? How are we going to compete with Ella and the Crown Crowd? How could I do this without using the stupid app? We have to write a speech and present it in front of the whole grade. But first we need a fun way to introduce ourselves to the 6th grade voting body and announce our candidacy.

My mom reluctantly approached us with a thought. "If I may? Why don't you do a Candy Gram? You could hand out M&Ms. Get it? Mollie and Marshall? M&M?"

"Ooooh, the kids would eat that up," I said.

"Literally," Mollie laughed.

"I'm ALL over that," Caden mumbled through a mouthful of cookies.

“Thanks, Campaign Manager Mom." I loved how creative my mom could be on the spot.

She went on to suggest we attach a note with a ribbon to the candy that said, “Come out of your Shell. Vote for M&M (Mollie and Marshall) for 6th Grade Co-Presidents and have a Sweet Year!”

I liked the sound of our names together.

Seriously, Marshall - Stop!

She insisted we somehow incorporate a tie-in to Share Faire, but I shot it down faster than a clay pigeon at the range. The candy grams are a great idea, and we ran with it like Kobe on a fast break up the court. We could give them out in the lobby before school and hit the sports games after school.

We got started right away and decided that fun size M&Ms would be best because, let’s be honest, we do not have unicorn money like some people. We could get them in bulk inexpensively since there had to be enough for 250 sixth graders and account for extras just in case. My mom is a bit deflated that her Share Faire idea was nixed but she still ran out to get the supplies for us.

Notes were created on the computer and, when she returned, attached to the candy using ribbon we found in our craft room. The ribbon read, "VOTE," so surely it must have been used in one of Ruby's previous races. We were ready, and for the first time, we were actually optimistic! *#RoseColoredGlasses*

The next day, there was a long table placed in the lobby for us to use. The lobby has a large circular shaped entrance that features floor to ceiling windows. The light poured in, and everything felt warm and toasty. The space was accessorized with plants, flowers in window boxes, pale cobalt blue walls, and shiny tiled floors. It was certainly the nicest part of Weston Middle. People in school referred to it as the Atrium. When I was little and came here for events, I called it the Aquarium because it felt as if you were floating inside a big fishbowl. *#Glub*

We displayed everything and said hello to our curious classmates. Being the lifesaver that she is, Mom also suggested making a sign to hang from the table that matched the theme of the candy grams, as well as a general information sheet about our campaign goals that students could grab quickly. We would go deeper into details when writing our campaign speech, so our initial plans were basic. As Co-Presidents we would:

Promote School Spirit

Promote Academic Excellence

Promote the importance of Participation (extracurricular activities)

Promote Leadership (especially in challenging times)

Promote Student Relations and Anti Bullying

Promote Inclusion for EVERYONE

As expected, the M&Ms were a big hit, and we reached a lot of students. What is it about candy that makes tweens lose their minds? Throughout the day, we witnessed people scarfing them down and talking a mile a minute about the election. Others were definitely feeling the effects of a pre-diabetic height and could crash at any moment! I didn't want to break my arm patting myself on the back too much, but maybe this can be done without relying on Share Faire.

After school, Mollie and I stopped by the athletic fields to hand out the remainder of the candy. We inhaled the cool autumn breeze as we canvassed the area. Leaves in deep shades of red, gold, and orange haphazardly fell on the turf. Most of the students wore the standard middle school uniform for this time of year.

For girls, it's oversized sweatshirts, leggings, scrunchies, and fuzzy socks. The boys wore hoodies and sporty shorts. Yes, shorts. Some boys even wore shorts in the middle of snowstorms. It's a whole scene. There is actually a method to the middle school dressing madness. If a girl likes a boy, she gives him her scrunchie and if he likes her back he wears it on his wrist. This let people know he was taken. On the flip side, if a boy was crushing over a girl, he would let her wear his hoodie. It was all in the official Middle School Crush Handbook.

Annie had a field hockey game and scored two goals. Good thing Principal Taylor let her slide on that argument with Ella. Annie was beast mode on and off the field. She could definitely hang with the boys. My sister "Sandra" was living up to her birth name. Sandra Day O'Connor once said, "The power I exert on the court depends on the power of my arguments, not my gender." The same could be said of Annie when she plays. Gender contrasts aside, she definitely has sports skills and is capable of Hurricane Sandy-level destruction of the competition. Who knew she could live up to that name too? *#HurricaneAnnie*

Mollie and I took in the action together, sitting close. Her shampoo smells like strawberries and at this moment, strawberries are my favorite thing in the entire world.

I was hanging out with a girl, and she didn't have cooties.

She is actually a riot and has a goofy side.

I studied her from head to toe and acknowledged, "You're way different than I thought."

"Different how?" she asked, bumping her shoulder to my shoulder, with an inquisitive brow raised.

"I don't know. Like, you are funny. I never knew you were so funny. I thought you just read books all day long and studied AP Calculus for amusement" I snickered.

"People think they know me, but few people do, ya know? she chuckled.

"Are you serious? Of course I know. People think they know me, but they have no clue." I added.

"No clue about what?" She seemed genuinely interested.

"About so much." I was vague. I actually had no idea what I was saying. I was trying not to look as dorky as I felt.

"Like this?" she pointed down to my Star Wars Baby Yoda socks. "What are THOSE?"

Slightly humiliated, I admitted, "Yeah, I'm a bit of a Star Wars Geek."

She surprised me when she recalled, "Remember in fourth grade, you dressed as Chewbacca for Halloween? Your mom's page views went through the roof that day."

I couldn't believe my ears, "You follow my mom's Share Faire page?"

"Sometimes," she confessed with a glow. "You were an adorable little baby."

My heart twisted in a knot.

We continued to share secrets while watching the game.

Mollie was telling me things that I never had any idea about:

1. She's quiet in school because she gets extremely anxious.
2. She learned to read at 18 months old and was fast tracked educationally starting in preschool. She feels the weight of expectations placed on her.
3. She's actually a year ahead in knowledge but her parents did not want her to skip a grade because of the socialization.
4. She wished she had a sibling.
5. All she really wants is a best friend. She has friends but not a true bestie.

In return, I rattled off some unknown Marshall facts:

1. Some old Share Faire videos make me cringe.
2. My dad really makes me feel pressured about the future.

3. I have no idea who I am outside of being Share Faire famous.

4. I wish my mom would stop posting.

5. Although surrounded by people, I often feel totally alone.

I've never been so open with a girl who wasn't Ruby. The flutters continued to show up uninvited. This could be a problem. Did I have a crush on Mollie Banks? Gives new meaning to "M&M." Should I give her my hoodie? Ugh. Caden! Caden always liked her first and I can't break Bro Code. I have to separate. She's Mollie, my friend and election partner. That's all it could be. Plus, I am not old enough or even ready for any of this. The flutters, however, were not convinced.

As for Ella, she had been pretty nonexistent all day. Actually, I don't remember seeing her in Social Studies this afternoon. She could be hunched over in a ball, crying in a corner because she didn't come up with the genius candy gram idea. Somehow, I knew better. That was not her style.

#UpToSomething

11

Early October | Ella's Royal Court

Without warning, there's a buzz around the school. No, seriously, we can actually hear vibrations of something. What on Earth is that sound? Oh no. Ella found an electrifying election theme of her own. Students were so stoked to play with their custom fidget spinners Ella had made. No doubt they came from her mom's graphic design firm. They were metallic in the shape of a crown and printed on each side were tiny jewels.

Ok Your Highness

It came with an invitation that said, "Stop Spinning in Circles. Follow the Crown Crowd and Rule the School. Join Ella's Royal COURT."

Oh no she did not!

She knew darned well I was named after a judge. Low blow.

Also printed on the invite was a QR code that students were to scan using their phone.

Oh dear goodness.

The QR code linked to a campaign video. It showed Ella in her house.

Or wait, was that a Palace?

No, it was definitely her house. In the video, she was showing everyone around, visiting each room, some which boasted cathedral ceilings and European inspired pillars. She explained how posh it would be to have school events and meetings at the estate. Clearly price is not an option in the Price House. *#Castle*

Could she do that? Phone bells were ringing left and right! The sounds of Christmas coming early.

The premise of the video was to promise popularity and grand entertainment to all who joined her court. Royal background violin music accompanied the tour. I must admit that it was tempting. Maybe Mom was right. I should use Share Faire to end this thing now.

Mollie sighed when she met me at my last class, “We are definitely in for a fight, Marshall. You still in?”

“Yup. Let’s meet at my house after school for an emergency meeting." I replied.

“Ok, but I have cello lessons so it will be after six, will that work?" she asked.

“Yeah, I’ll be there. See you then."

“Bye” she said as my stomach did a forward roll into a foam pit of feelings.

Speeches for the election were to take place next Thursday with the vote happening on Friday. We had a week to kick our campaign into high gear or allow our rear ends to get kicked.

The day was endless. Every time I heard the low hum of a fidget spinner my body contracted, and I was about to vomit. Just as I was fighting off the urge to purge, I caught sight of Ella. Seeing her turned me green. First, with envy over her snazzy campaign materials and then just with utter disgust. She pranced her way over. I braced myself.

“Did you get a spinner, Scary? Would hate for you to miss out on all of the fun. It’s not too late to concede, ya know. We all think you are past your prime anyway. I heard agents are casting for a live action stick figure project, you should go for that instead," she said mockingly.

I was done and so infuriated, the skin practically melted off my face, “Look Ella, you can sit up on your throne all you want. I will never bow down to you. You are not royalty, and I am not a quitter. I’m named after a Supreme

Court Justice who was considered an underdog his entire life. I still have some fight left."

Man, my dad would be satisfied!

"Suit yourself, Lolli. It's your precious time to suck, not mine."

She sashayed away as if she was on a fashion runway. That girl definitely got to me, and I wanted to take her down! *#DethroneTheQueen*

I darted home that afternoon and waited for Mollie to finish her cello lesson. She's in the Honors Orchestra and has rehearsals both in and out of school. Talented, funny, and more attractive with each slight change in hair color. In the summer, her hair is more ginger tinted but in the Fall, it's a deeper shade of red. It really makes her ivory skin and subtle freckles pop.

So many things about her to like.

STOP! Even thinking these things is like a betrayal to Caden. What would he do if he found out that I liked

Mollie? WOAH! I just admitted that I like Mollie. This may not end well. He's my friend. I want her to be more than a friend. Will any of these friendships survive this shift? A seismic earthquake of feelings cracks through my heart and I honestly do not think I can handle it right now. Emotional debris is everywhere! Between this and the campaign going off the rails, it's too much. I wandered aimlessly around the house trying to figure out a way to get momentum back for our campaign. Ella's video had been seen by all of the students at Weston, not just the sixth graders. There were even people in Annie's grade clambering to be a part of the royal court. The video was posted to multiple social media sites including Share Faire. While it was not yet at viral numbers, the likes continued to climb by the second, and it was seen by enough people who wanted to be a part of the hierarchy. *#Impressionable*

Ella was right. This was a big waste of time, but I did not have it in me to walk away. First of all, my parents would be extremely disappointed. I would certainly fail Ruby on some level. Finally, the competitive animal in Annie would chew me up and spit me out. All of this felt much more painful than just trying my best and losing with dignity. Or should we just use Share Faire? Before I could wallow any longer, a faint cry came from Ruby's room.

I rushed in to see her sitting in her swivel chair, sadder than a kid who dropped their ice cream. Two shiny college catalogs were on the desk and her head was in her hands. Coming up from behind, I wrapped my arms around her shoulders.

"Ruby, What's wrong?"

I don't think I have ever seen Ruby cry. She's so strong. Now Annie has cried but out of pure incense, not necessarily due to feelings.

Startled, she popped right up, wiping her cheeks, "Oh, hey Marsh. I didn't know you were here."

"You were crying. I heard you. What's going on?" I was concerned.

"It's nothing . . . everything . . . school . . . life." She let out a stray sniffle and her chest lifted up and down. She placed her hand just below her neck, inhaled sharply, and whooshed it out.

I needed to help her. And if I was being real, I needed her to help me too.

I leaned in and said, "Here's a game we can play. You tell me what's wrong and how I can help, then you can do the same for me."

Ruby played along.

"You need help, Bud? Why?" She carefully questioned.

"Nope you first. Those are the rules." I pressed.

"I guess I am just stressing about college." She picked up the two catalogs and flipped through the pages, stopping at sections that were marked with tiny sticky notes.

“My dream is to go to the University of the Arts and study Art Therapy. What better way to help kids by doing something I love so much? But then there is Dad who has been all over me about the University of Pennsylvania and their Law and Political Science Programs. He keeps saying that Art is not a real career, but I think it really can be. I have no idea how to convince him.”

I tried not to smirk too much after she was done. Relief came over me.

“Is it selfish of me to be thankful that both of these schools are located in the city of Philadelphia and only an hour drive away?” I asked, feeling a rush of guilt as the words left my mouth.

“No, not entirely selfish. Maybe a bit ill-timed since I’m still in mid-meltdown! But I want to be close to everyone for sure” she recognized.

“A thousand-pound elephant is sitting on my chest, and I can’t breathe when I talk to him. He wants me to pick a lane and I have; he just doesn't agree with the destination I'm driving to. Mom always stressed that our dreams should lead to our path and my dreams lately have been so vivid telling me what I need to do. My heart is in Art, Marsh."

"Holy wow, Ruby!" I said as I paged through the Art Therapy section in the Arts course catalog. "This is what you were meant to do. It's like they wrote this section with you in mind. You need to tell Dad how you feel. He's not the easiest person, I know, but you need to do it for you. You've worked so hard, and you deserve this."

She inhaled her doubts and exhaled her future goals into the universe as if to pray to the gods to give her strength to tell Dad. She then changed the subject, "Well, thanks. Enough about me. What's up with you? Why are you sulking all around the house looking like a lost puppy?"

It was the moment of truth. Time to lay it all out there for my sister, and even myself, to know what I've known for the past month. To finally say it out loud.

"I like Mollie Banks. Like really like her, like her." My hands flew over my face as if I couldn't believe I finally admitted it to myself. "But I'm pretty sure Caden likes her too and even liked her first. I can't break Bro Code. Not to mention this election is snowballing into an avalanche level of disaster. Ella's video is almost at viral numbers and Mom has been on me to use Share Faire. I am completely lost and don't know what to do. I want to do my own thing, be my own person, not rely on being a former famous baby for the rest of my life. UGGGHHHHHH." The frustration crashed over me like a rogue wave.

"Marsh, you need to go back to the weekend before school started," Ruby explained.

I was not following.

“Remember how nervous you were? What did you want more than anything?” she asked.

“Besides knowing who wrote the note? I don't know, I guess for people to know me, the real me, and to feel comfortable," I replied.

She went on, “Well, who are you?

Caught off guard, I questioned, “Who Am I?”

“Yes, who is Marshall Hope?” she pushed.

“I’m a person who tries to do my best and is friendly to everyone. I love soccer, my dog, and care about my friends and family. I try to do what is right, not necessarily the easy thing.”

She looked at me in a way where I knew I was not going to like what she was about to say. My heart immediately sank. #*Heartbreak*

“Marsh, you need to let your feelings for Mollie go, at least for the time being. It’s not easy, I know. You can’t let a crush derail you from the main goal, which is to do the right thing - for everyone. I know Caden has never admitted out loud that he likes Mollie, but you KNOW he does. It would not be right to chase it.

Things will get very complicated, and things will change very fast. Your heart will eventually heal and recover but a betrayal of friendship likely will not. Not to mention, you are waaay too young for any of this. You have so much time."

She was right. I'm freaking twelve! I have years of heartache ahead of me, why start now? I wish I was more convinced though.

Ruby changed the subject, "What else, Marsh? Who do you want to be? Mr. Bloom and his gold standard of speeches on the future of life still haunt me to this day!"

"Oh my god, me too," my eyes bulged out of my head at her declaration and then I replied to her question, "I want to be someone who leads by example. I am not a follower or an Internet fad. I want people to know me - the person, not the hashtag."

Ruby answered back, "Ok. Now can you imagine being any of those things and fitting in under a President who essentially is a tyrant and makes empty promises based on popularity and status?"

"I never thought about it like that," I declared.

"You need to base your campaign on reality. What can you offer the students that matters?" she asked.

"I suppose we can tell everyone that we will listen to them, that we will be on their side as partners not bosses. It is our goal that all students feel included and involved in everything we hope to achieve."

"THAT's it!" she exclaimed. "Hope!"

Confused, I uttered, "Okaaaay . . ."

She cut me off, "Hope Banks. You need to set up Hope Banks in each 6th grade hallway. Give the students an opportunity to express what they want and need privately, without social pressure. People want to be heard, not bought."

Still confused, I asked, "Sounds good but what exactly are Hope Banks?

"You and Mollie, silly." Ruby's smile, as she spoke that sentence, was like being let in on a little secret.

She went downstairs to our craft room and proceeded to put together four "Hope Banks" to set up in each of the four sixth grade hallways. On them were instructions to anonymously share their hopes, goals, and suggestions for the school year on little pieces of green paper and then deposit them into the banks. We would review the boxes weekly and base our action plans on what the students tell us they want, not what we tell them.

Mollie arrived shortly thereafter, and she loved the idea of the "Hope Banks." We drafted our speech around this idea and prepared to offer the sixth-grade students at

Weston a Student Council run by people who support them, not a person who steamrolls them. *#Goals*

I certainly had a solution to my problems. I was not unsure of who I was anymore. I am a leader, not just a former famous baby. School is hard enough. Pretending to be something that I am not only harms intentions. I want to lead by example in every aspect and inspire people to do the same. I am picking my lane. Yet, first, I needed to take a detour.

"Hey Mollie?" I quietly said.

"Yeah?" she replied.

"Can I ask you something? It's not election related. It's kind of personal, actually?" My jaw twitched at the change in vibe.

"Um, sure. I guess so.." Her green eyes opened with anticipation.

What am I doing?

"Are you allowed to date?" As the words left my mouth, I wished for a net to catch them and scoop them back in!

"Well, the situation has really never come up. I think my parents would be ok with a movie or something, as long as they know the boy. Why are you asking, exactly?" She looked hopeful with a bashful smile turning upwards. My heart sank like the Titanic knowing what I needed to do.

"What do you think about Caden?" I suggested.

Doing the right thing was more important than hurting people I care about the most. At that moment, I had to let Mollie go in my mind . . . my heart would catch up, right? Our story might not be totally over, but it is for now. Our future will sort it out in years to come. I could certainly fulfill the duties of being her BFF for now, a true bestie. *#Crushed*

However, I was still troubled about how Dad would react to Ruby's plans for the future. She was the first-born, an overachiever, and someone who dad saw a glimmer of his younger self in. It would not be an easy conversation but one that is necessary.

12

October | Share Faire Farewell?

It's been a completely emotionally exhausting day and all I want to do is retreat into my comfy bed, pull the covers over my head, and pass out. Tomorrow is election day and I need to get some rest.

Lugging heavy legs to my room, the light of the computer coming from mom's office lit up the otherwise dark hallway. Peeking through the doorway, she sat with a fierce look of determination on her face. It was only when I realized what she was doing that my stomach lurched and resounding rage blurred my vision.

Outlined on the computer with animated M&Ms was the makings of a Share Faire campaign post. "The candy is out of the bag!" The blinking cursor mocked me as "Mollie and Marshall for President" flashed on the screen. My mom sat at the chair playing around with fonts, unaware that I was hovering and wanted to thrash her and the entire office.

I stormed through the door, and she nearly hit her head on the ceiling, she jumped so high.

"WHAT IS THIS?" my voice raised and bounced off the walls.

"I thought I said NO Share Faire! Why would you do this? Is it posted?"

Fury continued to build like a skyscraper on fire, smoldering from the bottom up. Mom's face fell and she slammed her laptop shut but it was too late.

"I saw Ella's video trending, so I just thought you needed a boost."

Was she actually trying to justify her actions?

"I told you over and over I wanted to do this without Share Faire. Why can't you understand? I'm done with you using me as your puppet for likes. Do you have any idea how hard it's been for me lately? Never knowing if someone likes me for me or if it's some desperate attempt for click bait? You did this. From the time I was a toddler, you did this. Now I'm done! Delete that and don't use my picture again. Stay out of my life!"

Looking stunned, tears formed in the corner of Mom's eyes, "Marshall I'm …."

I cut her off before she had a chance to finish.

"No. It's over. I'm not a baby anymore. I need to make my own mark."

Mom tried to get words out through broken sobs, "Everything I do, I do for you and your sisters. I never, ever wanted you to feel the pain I felt. I . . . I just wanted to help."

I popped off even more!

“I don’t need your help. I need you to leave me alone!”

I nearly broke every step on the way up to my room. I crashed headfirst into my bed and buried my face in the pillow. My mind was screaming. I never yelled at mom like that. Through the door I heard muffled sniffles and voices carrying.

I got up and slammed the door so hard I was certain it was coming off the hinges. The windows clattered, heavy footsteps barged, and a shadow appeared under my door frame.

Imagine my surprise when it was Dad, not Mom looming in the doorway. That’s it. Rest In Peace Marshall. After the way I spoke to her, Dad really will ground me until 46 or bury my body in the backyard. *#RIP*

But he sat on the edge of my bed and shocked me by rubbing the sensitive area between my shoulders. All my tension lives there so it was nice to have dad knock the knots out.

"Marshall you have to understand she was going to post it but thought better of it. All she wants is the best for you and your sisters. Unconditional love makes you lose yourself every now and again. She never meant to betray your trust. Ever."

Biting my quivering lip and trying to hide how sorry I was, "I know. It's just all too raw. The election, Mom, Share Faire, Mollie. I'm buried under a million pounds of feelings that won't budge. It's like I'm in quicksand and no one can help fish me out. The more I try to maneuver my way around, the more stuck I become. My life is slipping under and then I slowly drown beneath the surface."

Dad looked utterly shocked at my verbal diarrhea. "Yeah - wow, that's a lot . . . Look, it was all just a misunderstanding. You know your mom cares about your wishes and respects the path you want to take, that's all she's ever wanted, you know. For you to pick a path and stay in your lane on the road to happiness. That's what we both want."

"I know. I'll talk to her." The overwhelming guilt about the way I spoke to her was suffocating.

It was official. I've drawn a line in the sand. My relationship with Share Faire is over unless I want it to be. Mom is done controlling my image online for likes. I've struggled with this for so long. Who am I without fame? I guess I am about to find out. I'd be lying if I said I wasn't a little bit nervous but also excited. It's time for me to be me . . .whoever that is. But for now, I'm tired and need to sleep on all of this.

I need to be alone. Alone with my thoughts. Alone with my plans. Alone in my bed. It's late and it's a huge day tomorrow. I really was not expecting so much Drama-Rama to go down tonight of all nights. But I guess everything happens for a reason. There is a reason I am in the place that I am in and someday it will all make sense. I just wish that day would come sooner rather than later.

Just one more thing to do before I put this awful evening out with the trash,

“And Dad, you might want to practice what you preach?”

Dad looked at me like I had twelve heads, “What do you mean?”

“Have you talked to Ruby lately?" I asked.

13

October | Speech Day

Speech day is here! A mahogany podium is set up in the middle of the gym and there are silver folding chairs on both sides of it for us to sit. Pine floor cleaner, rubber basketballs, and the faint odor of socks hung in the gym air. The midnight blue bleachers were filled with blaring sixth graders who couldn't sit still long enough to notice Principal Taylor trying to get everyone's attention. Waving a hand desperately yet in vain, her voice echoed off of the rafters. She stilled and eventually everyone else followed suit.

She then spoke eloquently into the microphone,

"Boys and Girls. We are here today to meet the candidates for your 6th grade Student Council. Please pay attention to each speech and decide which person is the best fit for each job. It is a great responsibility to be on the Student Council and make a commitment to represent your peers. I applaud all of the brave students sitting up here and thank them for their interest in making our school the best it can be. Without further ado, meet the candidates."

Clapping

My stomach was upside down like Simone on Vault. In hindsight, it was probably not the best idea to have a stuffed meatball sub and double fudge brownie, washed down with a cherry icee for lunch. Caden's influence! My tummy feels like a rock spinning in a laundry machine.

The order of speeches has the Secretary candidates present first, followed by Treasurer, Vice President, and finally the President nominees. Ruby's voice is in my head on repeat, "Offer them something that matters."

Ella is dressed up in a designer sweater dress that flashes the logo boldly on the front. Her blonde hair is slicked back into a sleek tight bun, held in place with a sparkling crystal pin. She's also wearing the fancy boots she had on the first time she heavily trudged up and bit my head off at the lockers. She started her speech and, as expected, it was a commercial to join the Crown Crowd. Promises of meetings in the luxurious pool and hot tub at her castle mansion were made.

Principal Taylor actually had to interrupt at one point to tell her that was not allowed. "Ella, stick to the facts of the campaign please," she lectured.

Ella was not deterred. Cool, calm, and collected, she continued:

"Listen, everyone. I know what you all want and need. It is the same thing I and the other members of the Crown

Crowd want: to have power, to make decisions that are best for us, and to command respect. If I am elected, I will take this office very seriously and be a President who moves through what everyone wants - social fun. Sure, it would be great to be able to join a book club or get visits from local authors. But we all know that is not what kids in middle school want. We want crazy trips, we want events, we want parties, and we want popularity. And we want access to our phones all the time! As members of the court, we usually get what we want!"

Continuing . . .

"Still, social status is not for everyone. We have hierarchies in this country for a reason and I believe our school Student Council should have them too. There are people who are born to lead, like me, while others are destined to follow, like some scary people. It is just the way things are. We need a class system so everyone knows their place. Will you get a vote under my council? Of course.

Does it mean that we will automatically accept it? Of course not. But trust that, I am super determined to make sure everyone has at least a chance to live out their middle school dreams."

I could see the wheels of the student body turning. Oohs and aaahs of the little people played tug of war as the drivers of the school were in control.

When she was finished, she handed the microphone to Mollie and sneered, "Good luck following that, Peasants." *#MicDrop*

Mollie stood before the group without pausing. If her nerves were wreaking havoc, she did not show it. She spoke first and elaborated on the bullet points we initially noted in our M&M campaign flier. She was soft spoken; yet firm in what she was saying. There was no doubt that Mollie was convinced of how qualified we would be to lead the 6th Grade class. Caden is in the stands staring at her with lovesick googly eyes. He was locked in. The irony is not lost on me. He is crushing on Mollie's presence, the way most girls in our grade are crushing on his. I wanted my friend to be happy. He needs to tell her how he feels. *#Ship*

It was almost my turn where I was to speak about the "Hope Banks." While Mollie was talking about what we wanted to promote, it was my job to explain how we would promote and why it mattered to elect us. No small feat.

Mollie winked adorably as I walked up to the podium. I nearly tripped on the cords at the gesture, but I made it without face planting in front of the entire grade. I took my place and traced the microphone lightly with my finger, then tapped it to make sure it worked. The sound reverberated sending shock waves through the crowd.

"Hello, my name is Marshall Goode Hope and along with Mollie Banks, we are running for Co-Presidents of the Sixth Grade. You've heard from Mollie about what we want to do for you all, but I am here to talk to you about what everyone wants to do. How can we share fair?"

There was a heavy gasp at this loaded declaration. The kids were shaken and began squealing with surprised jubilation. Principal Taylor made her best efforts to shush everyone. Mollie's eyes were wide saucers of disbelief.

Was I really going to use Share Faire to steal this election? Was I about to stoop to Ella's level? Was I about to take the easy way out to win? What about my future and Mr. Bloom?

Once everyone regained composure, I continued, "You all know me as the Share Faire Kid. Because my mom paraded me on the internet as a baby and everyone in this room basically watched me grow up online, you probably think you know me. The easiest thing for me to do is to promise all of you shout outs and followers that would give you the viral Share Faire fame that you all crave."

More cheering

Putting my hand up to a stop, I commanded their attention, "But I'm sorry to say, if you think I am going to do that, you don't know me at all."

Mollie revealed a radiant grin. She knew what was coming next.

"I am named after the great Supreme Court Justice Thurgood Marshall. I may not know as much about him as my dad does, but one thing I do know is he would never take the easy way out. He was a debater by nature. He challenged logic at every turn and proved every statement he made. He did not care about fame or wealth. Justice Thurgood Marshall held everyone to a higher moral standard and so does former Justice Marshall Hope."

Everyone stared at me FULL STOP in silence.

"I am officially done with Share Faire. Fame and popularity is not the answer to middle school problems. Being a keyboard warrior and broadcasting what you think behind the safety net of a screen is not real life. Bullying, whether online or face-to-face, serves no purpose. It's awful and cruel. Eventually, we will need to learn to talk to each other, speak to each other nicely, even when the conversations are tough. Guys, this is Middle School. It's all tough. But if we say what we mean and mean what we say, in person, with kindness, we can maybe change things starting now." *#CoolToBeKind*

(Bloom's Basics Number 3 - Respect yourself and others too).

"It's true when I say I want everyone to share fair, but not in the way you think. You may have noticed the 'Hope Banks' placed throughout the Sixth-Grade wing. Well, that was our way to make you share fairly. Share your ideas and your hopes. Share your fears or your worries. Just know that whatever you share will be read with care by Mollie and me. We want to hear your voices and offer to you Student Council experiences that matter. We want to learn, we want writers to come visit us, we want to be able to have STEM clubs and try to be the best we can be. And of course, we want fun stuff too, but it is important to be well rounded people and that is part of our focus as potential Presidents."

Breathe

"So please, before you vote tomorrow, be sure to drop your green notes in the banks and know we will always listen and strive to help you, in the fairest way possible. You matter, your vote counts, you deserve a standard like the real Justice Marshall, and we will prove it to you!" *#FTW*

Thunderous applause broke out across the gym. Ella's face dropped and it suddenly occurred to her that she was not going to reign supreme uncontested. Yet, she still held her nose to the sky and barely looked our way. No offerings of good luck, congratulations on a race well run, or superficial small talk. Ella was stoic in her ignorance. Mollie and I ran a noble campaign, fit for a King and

Queen. All we could do now was wait to see how the middle school political wars would play out. #*Redemption*

14

October | Election Day

Election Day is finally here. Voting would be done in the morning and counted by lunchtime. Another assembly would take place in the afternoon where the winners would be announced to the entire sixth grade class.

The parents and siblings of all of the candidates were invited to the ceremony and to a small reception afterwards. This was a time-honored tradition that Weston did to congratulate everyone who ran in the election, not just the winners. I have been to three of them recognizing Ruby's time on the Student Council. My favorite part was the food, especially the cheeseboards. So much cheese!

#CheeseHead

The ride to school was unusually quiet. Only the background noise of the radio was heard. My mom knew I was a trainwreck but did not want to push, especially after our fight the other night. Leave it to Annie to push.

"Good luck today, Marsh."

What? She never called me that.

"Thanks Annie." I paused. "But I think it will be close."

"You dealt with that wicked witch a lot better than I ever could. I hope she falls off her broom and then melts into a scorching pile of Chanel candle wax when you win."

My mom hiccupped, swallowing a belly laugh within and added, "Well, we will all be there later today and are proud of you no matter what. You never lost sight of who you are and that is to be celebrated."

She let out another "Good luck Hun," as we climbed out of the car.

I turned back though, “Hey Mom.”

“Are you ok Marshall?” she replied with concern.

“I’m sorry." I whispered.

“I know. Me too, hun. Go get em’, ok!" she urged.

“I will. See ya later.” I felt better already.

Walking through the front doors of the building was different today. I am who I have always been but through this process, I discovered parts of myself that were hidden for whatever reason. Now, I feel like my fellow students finally know the real me. I’m not Justice Marshall. I am not a meme. I am just like them, a little lost and a lot awkward. I’m a person trying to figure out weird feelings and attempting to find my place in the world. I hope the words I spoke yesterday made sense.

Maybe leading a social change party by bringing people together through poppin’ preaching can be my “thing." Follow your own path. It's the key to unlocking your dreams.

Passing by one of the “Hope Banks," I hastily grabbed a pen and jotted, “I hope I matter. I hope I can make a difference. I hope I can do what is right." I stuffed my paper in the box that was already overflowing with wrinkled notes.

Homeroom was extended so everyone had a chance to cast his or her vote. It was a super long morning. The teachers had a hard time keeping rambunctious kids focused in the first half of classes since there was so much conversation and jitters surrounding the election. Trying to concentrate was an exercise in Jedi mind training. I don't even think Yoda could get me to comply. *#UseTheForce*

After lunch, we all ran around the recess yard to get the wiggles out. It kind of reminded me of my family’s trips to the park, though this time without a panic attack!

Anything to get me moving should help keep my mind off the worry I have over the final tally. Battles in the Gaga pit and a game of “infection” did the trick. Most of the 6th graders were running around like maniacs and enjoying the movement break. Ella and the Crown Crowd congregated by the door and were surely plotting someone's demise . . . probably mine. Whether we were dodging balls or dodging barbs, we are sixth graders who are all in this together.

It's finally 2:30! The teachers are corralling restless students to the gym. They occupied the hard bleachers as they did the day before but instead of the lively spirit on display during the speeches, the tense fog in the room was much thicker today. You could cut it with a lightsaber. Who won? By the day's end, everyone was pretty impatient. They just wanted to know. *#TellUsNow*

Principal Taylor took her usual position at the podium and started the proceedings. The candidates were sitting in the same chairs as yesterday but off to the right, there were more chairs set aside for the families of the candidates. Mom, Dad, Ruby, and Annie were seated together. Mom waved, Dad nodded, Ruby gave a thumbs up, and Annie stuck her tongue out playfully in my direction, which helped lighten the mood.

One by one candidates were recognized, and winners announced. Hugs and smiles engulfed the gymnasium. It was finally our turn. Mollie and I stood together united and turned to face Ella Price.

Principal Taylor announced, “This Presidential Election was one of the closest races we have ever seen here at Weston; 52 percent to 48 percent. Congratulations to all of you for your time and effort in the name of serving your fellow classmates.”

My heart was beating out of my chest. Mollie’s stomach grumbled. Ella was cold as ice.

Principal Taylor concluded, “I am pleased to announce the presidential election winner of Weston Middle School sixth grade is . . . Co-Presidents Mollie Banks and Marshall Hope."

What in the name of all that is holy? *#SHOCKED*

Walking on a cloud of victory, Mollie and I could not help ourselves. Chants of “M&M, M&M” played on a loop and we jumped for joy! We actually won. My family beamed with pride. Mollie’s mom and dad were there too, proud of their daughter. Ella’s disappointment gutted me, which is a shock to me too. For the first time all year, I actually saw her have genuine emotion. I looked towards the family section but did not see anyone who could be her parents.

Did she not have anyone here for her?

The students went back to class for dismissal and the newly elected Student Council, their fellow nominees, and families were invited to the cafeteria for the reception. On his way out, Caden gave a congratulatory pat on the back and reminded me to save him some Gouda and Colby jack cheese. That was an oddly specific request.

#FoodComaCaden

As he was walking away, I got my nerve up and called out, “Caden, wait a sec!”

“Yeah, what’s up, did you forget my order already?” he teased.

“No." Reluctantly, I swallowed hard and came right out with it, “You should tell her."

“Tell who, what?” he asked cluelessly.

“Caden, it’s obvious to anyone with eyesight that you like Mollie. I can see why. She’s really great." I confessed.

“Are you an Eye Doctor now? No way. I don't like Mollie, you are way off base," he resisted uncomfortably.

“Wait . . . do YOU like her? Did something happen," he tried to stay cool, but he was doing a terrible job. His hair was practically upright from messing with it so roughly.

“Man, come on - I am your best friend, I know you. Nothing happened because YOU like her. You look at her the way you look at food, like you can’t get enough. Listen, don’t be an idiot, she is too special to let pride or fear get in your way. Just think about it."

Growing serious and trying not to make eye contact, he replied, “Ok. Thanks, Bro. Maybe I will."

Clearly, I AM an Eye Doctor now! *#BroCode*

I was about to leave but saw Ella, still sitting in her seat in the middle of the empty gym. I motioned to everyone that I would catch up. Approaching Ella, I couldn't help but feel a little sorry for her. Her parents were nowhere to be found, the Crown Crowd was now absent, and she was all alone with her head down looking at the hardwood floor. The surge of sympathy certainly caught me off guard. This girl had essentially tortured me for two months, was the epitome of evil, yet I felt the need to do the right thing. Life Lessons that I actually remembered!

Get out of my head, Mr. Bloom!

“Ella," I proceeded with caution. “Are you alright?”

(Bloom's Basics Number 4 - Win with grace, lose with grace)

For the first time ever she spoke to me like a person. "I guess. It was a close race, but you won fair and square."

Looks like losing with grace is on her list too.

"Thanks. Are you coming to the reception? You deserve to be there as much as anyone else," I admitted.

"Why bother? My parents could not even show up for me today. They are always busy with work. My dad is barely home; he's always in the city. Half of the time the only way I can get anyone's attention is by acting out. Why do you think I am the way I am here, Marshall?"

Holy Heck. She didn't call me Scary. I honestly had no idea . . .

She went on, "Because it's a fool-proof way to be noticed. No one notices me at home, ever. But when I started acting like an entitled queen at school and using my parents' wealth as collateral, people wanted to be my friend. No one actually knows me."

My eyes squeezed shut and I leaned my head to one side in disbelief, "Ella, no one understands that more than I do."

"I know," she said, "You made great points about that throughout the campaign. You are actually inspiring people to be themselves. It's probably why you won. People want to be seen and feel like they really belong."

I could not believe it. I was having an actual conversation with Ella Price, and I didn't feel the overwhelming desire to run into oncoming traffic.

"Ella, the race was so close. That means there are a bunch of students who believed in what you stood for. You might not have gone about it the best way" I said, twitching my nose, "but the students do want gatherings and a chance to be a part of something special. I have an idea. I would have to run it by Mollie and get it approved by the Student

Council club advisor, but would you be interested in working with us, as Social Secretary?"

Ella smiled, a true whole face smile where her makeup wasn't the only thing sparkling. "You would do that for me?"

"Yes, you certainly have the event planning thing mastered and we could absolutely use your help with fun for everyone. What do you think?"

With a flick of the wrist, her index finger pointed up to her invisible crown, oh geez, but instead of adjusting it, she pretended to throw it away. *#ByeQueen*

"I'm in," she said.

We made our way to reception by walking side by side. It was vibrant in the cafeteria, and everyone was in good spirits. A mix of sandwiches, dessert trays, and the highly sought after cheeseboards were enjoyed by all. I brought everyone up to speed regarding what happened. Ella was super apologetic and let out a regretful apology, a release of a hundred different feelings. Mollie along with her family, my parents, and sisters - even Annie - agreed to welcome Ella to our table with open arms. *#BeTheBiggerPerson*

My mom's face softened a little. For our entire existence, she had no tolerance for bullying. None. She had suffered at the hands of bullies throughout her childhood and was deeply wounded inside because of it. But seeing this side of Ella; vulnerable and kind of broken, made her realize that sometimes bullying is more about the bully and less about who they harass.

There was nothing wrong with my mother. There was something very wrong with her bullies. This realization was finally comforting to her.

Mom and I are also in a much better place after our fight. Unless I want to someday have a Share Faire account of my own, which is something I am working out internally, she promised to be done with anything related to “Justice Marshall," even if it means losing some freelance work as a result. Her intent has always been to protect us so we would never have to feel any of the sadness she experienced growing up and this was her way of showing me.

Throughout the function, we sat and talked nonstop. We joked with jovial laughter and ate plenty of delicious cheese. By evening's end, the behavior of the last two months was forgiven, and we scheduled our first unofficial meeting for the next weekend to be held at my house.

(Bloom's Basics Number 5 - Forgiveness is important and a secret ingredient in the recipe for happiness).

As twelve-year olds, we were pretty mature! We made the choice to move on, so we could move ahead, together. We did not do what was easy, we did what was right. Thurgood Marshall would be proud. *#AllGrownUp*

15

November | Winners and the Return of Share Faire

Before we even had time to enjoy our win, it was time to meet for the first time as Student Council Officers. Excited, I skipped every other step on my way downstairs around 10:00 am. Wiping the crust from my eyes after a full night of restful sleep, I feel really good about having the newly elected sixth grade Student Council at my house to have a prep meeting.

Rounding the corner to the kitchen, I had to look twice to see what was happening. Are my eyes playing tricks on me? The nook was boldly decorated in patriotic red, white, and blue which just so happened to correspond to Weston's school colors. Plates, cups, and napkins were stacked on the table next to a roll of "I Voted" stickers. Balloons and streamers in the same shade consumed the room. On each chair was a personalized notebook for each Student Council member. My mom was a boss!

"Mom," I said blinking rapidly. "This is so awesome."

Proud of herself, she noted "You know I could not let an occasion like this go by without doing something!"

Annie was still asleep (we likely would not see her until at least noon). Dad and Ruby were in Philadelphia for the weekend. They had their talk about Ruby's college plans and dad agreed to accompany her on visits to both schools. He vowed to keep an open mind throughout the entire process and trust the fine young lady he helped raise. Ruby was his shining star in the constellation of life, so deep down he knew success would be hers no matter which path she chose. It was certainly a breakthrough moment that I could not help but take a little credit for. *#GirlDad*

My friends burst into the house and were super pumped up about the election decor. Elation came over the group when mom took a cake out of the fridge. It is a masterfully decorated vanilla cake, covered in buttercream icing and had strawberries and blueberries that were arranged to match Weston's official school logo. I'm practically drooling, it looked almost too good to eat. As if on cue, there was a sound at the door. KNOCK KNOCK KNOCK

"CADEN," I called. "You are just in time." I invited him to join to give us a student point of view since he volunteered to be his homeroom representative. In addition to helping keep his class in the Student Council loop, there was food at the meetings and he's always ravenous. Plus, it's another way to get closer to Mollie. It was then that I detected something on his wrist . . . Gray and white polka dots . . .

Wait! Was he wearing her scrunchie? OMG!

#MiddleSchoolCrushHandbook

Everyone took a seat around the kitchen table. Our first item on the to-do list is to review all of the notes in the "Hope Banks." I took the four boxes and proceeded to dump the green notes on the table. I shook the box and the last of the notes flew out. It was way cool to have these little pieces of insight on what the sixth graders of Weston wanted and needed in order to make their first year of middle school the best ever.

"I want to get to know more people," one note said.

"Please organize a student vs. teacher basketball game," said another.

The notes got more personal, "It is important that I have chances to grow at school and be happy."

I spoke up, "Based on most of the feedback, we should definitely plan some sort of dance so all of our classmates could get to know each other outside of the classroom."

"Any ideas," I challenged the group.

A hand shot up like a rocket.

Oh right.

“Handing the floor over to our newly appointed Social Secretary," I directed in my most presidential tone.

Ella Price sat straight up, shoulders back, and shimmied in her chair. Self-assured, there was something different about her as she confidently shared her plan.

“No dance. We are going to have a Share Faire instead!”

Mouths fell open. Agape with no escape! Here we go again! Almost giddy, she went on, “Yup, a Share Faire. A festival for the sixth-grade class filled with games, a dunk tank for the teachers, contests, silly dances, and mindless fun. Just like the app but unplugged!”

It was an absolutely perfect idea. We could have it at the park. The amphitheater was just begging for rowdy sixth graders to stomp the stage.

I threw the suggestion to the council for our first vote, “Everyone in favor of a Sixth Grade Share Faire, say I."

The group responded with a resounding and unanimous, "I".

"Ok then, I said, "Let's get to work."

#MiddleSchoolRules

The mid-November weather gods were on our side. The trees had nearly lost all of their leaves, but their branches looked sculpted like a ballerina's stretched pose. Birds were still chirping about. We had a simply gorgeous late Autumn Saturday for our First Annual Weston Sixth Grade Share Faire Fest.

Stations were set up throughout the grounds of the park. We were able to secure the Amphitheater too. The strings of lights flickered against the backdrop of a late Fall afternoon, highlighting the indigo skies and gray clouds. The sun shined on and off over the course of the day which made for a comfortable warmth and feel throughout the air. Scents of Smores toasting on wood logs and nearby fireplaces blazing was another layer of delight.

Students, parents, and teachers visited each themed booth. We were able to coordinate a fun list of activities for everyone to enjoy:

1. Station 1 - Mindfulness. Yoga with Puppies. (Michael Jordan has no zen, so he sat out).

2. Station 2 - Music. Karaoke on the Amphitheater Stage.

3. Station 3 - Dance. Moonbounce Hip Hop Dance Party.

4. Station 4 - Art. Ruby's Face Painting and Chalk the Walk with Positive Thoughts.

5. Station 5 - Games. Chess, Checkers, Scrabble.

6. Station 6 - Sports. Gaga, Soccer, and Stick Handling lessons with Annie (if you dare!)

7. Station 7 - Waterworks. Teacher Dunk Tank and Water Balloon Toss.

8. Station 8 - FUN-draising. Share Fair Cares Booth. Donate funds or your new or gently used items to benefit underprivileged students in our district.

9. Station 9 - Share Faire Photo and Video Booth. Hashtag your posts with *#WestonShareFaireFest*

10. Station 10 - Hope Banks Box Challenge - Write down your hopes for the next Sixth Grade Get Together and deposit them in the banks.

In addition to the booths, there were carnival type food trucks present (even the "Nine Juan Juan Taco Truck" made an appearance). Everyone floated through the day: drinks, bubbles, kites, conversation, and the spark of new friendships forming.

I proudly walked the event with Mollie and Ella at each side. I could not believe how far we had come. A few short months ago, we were competitors. Some of us were not even close to being friends. Some of us felt like we were more than a friend, a missing piece of a long-lost puzzle.

But this day, today, we were a perfect example of Mr. Bloom's last Life Lesson on the list:

And before I could get the words out, "Forgiveness is a secret ingredient…"

Caden came running. "Secret ingredient in what? I'm starving!"

In unison, Mollie, Ella, and I sang out with snark, "What else is new?"

Caden linked his arm with Mollie's, and they strolled together. It pinched my heart, but we were all having such a fun time, so I pushed those feelings away.

But to answer Caden's question, I found the words:

"Forgiveness is a secret ingredient in the recipe for a happy life, Dude. Sprinkle that stuff everywhere!"

Our futures are safe.

#Endgame

THE END

Acknowledgements

There are so many people who I would like to thank. First and foremost, thank you to my agent Andrea Comparato, of Inscriptions Literary, for believing in me and this project. You have spent countless hours in my corner and I appreciate everything you have done for me and my work.

Thank you to Oh MG Press for taking a chance on me and my story.

Thank you to Matthew Witt for the fabulous cover art that perfectly captured the vibe of the book.

Thank you to Franklin and the "Daugh Fam" from Tik Tok/Instagram. Franklin was my muse for this story and I loved imagining what he could do with his baby fame when he grows up! His inspiration brought my ideas to life.

To my friends, family, and online universe of supporters - your kind words and encouragement filled me on days where I ran on empty.

Thank You to Lorna Doucette who was my first ever "kid" reader of this story and who provided valuable feedback to make it what it is today.

A special shout out to Bethany Hensel who provided editorial feedback on this manuscript, as part of a Twitter contest. Your insight and comments elevated my words and took the story to another level.

Thank you to Kelly and Jodi for being my lifelong friends.

Thank you to my kids and their friends for showing me what real Middle and High School friendships are all about.

About the Author

Stephanie lives with her family in West Chester, Pennsylvania, but is originally from Central, New Jersey, where she has a degree in Communications and a Publishing and Professional Writing Certificate from Rider University. She is also a member of SCBWI (Eastern PA Chapter) & was a 2024 SCBWI Virtual Conference Scholarship winner.

Her poetry compilation, *Poems Stuck in my Head* was released in affiliation with Experiments in Fiction and reached Number One New Release in Children's Poetry on Amazon (ebook). *No School, My Rules* her debut picture book was published by Tielmour Press.

Stephanie identifies with underrepresented creators with chronic illnesses through her battle with the auto immune disease, Psoriatic Arthritis.

Finally, she enjoys reading, theatre, mindless web searching, Netflix binges, sunflowers, sports, and anything related to coffee.

Milton Keynes UK
Ingram Content Group UK Ltd.
UKHW021029270524
443319UK00017B/1026

9 798869 193070